Are you a small-business owner trying to find a better system for keeping track of your finances?

Are you a student having problems learning French?

Do you spend far too much time retyping correspondence, reports, or articles?

Would you like a good opponent for a game of chess, or do you want to singlehandedly save Earth from alien invaders?

Whatever your needs and interests, COMPUTERS FOR EVERYBODY can help you find the personal computer that will fill the bill. From the step-by-step method of choosing and buying a computer, to finding service and support systems, to tapping into the best sources of free, or almost free, software, this is your complete introduction to the world of personal computing. Whether you want to spend $300 or $3000, you'll find information on what is currently available, the pluses and minuses of each computer, and what hidden costs can turn a seemingly inexpensive system into a major investment. Whether you have already decided that you are going to join the computer age, or you're still trying to figure out what it's all about, here is the book that will answer your questions and resolve all your doubts—

COMPUTERS
FOR EVERYBODY

Explore the World of Computers with SIGNET

COMPUTERS
FOR
EVERYBODY

BY

Jerry Willis and Merl Miller

A SIGNET BOOK
NEW AMERICAN LIBRARY
TIMES MIRROR

Published by arrangement with dilithium Press

SIGNET TRADEMARK REG. U.S. PAT. OFF. AND FOREIGN COUNTRIES
REGISTERED TRADEMARK—MARCA REGISTRADA
HECHO EN CHICAGO, U.S.A.

SIGNET, SIGNET CLASSIC, MENTOR, PLUME, MERIDIAN and NAL
BOOKS are published by The New American Library, Inc., 1633 Broadway,
New York, New York 10019

First Signet Printing, September, 1983

1   2   3   4   5   6   7   8   9

When we decided to write this book, we started by defining our typical reader. We both wanted to keep someone in mind while we wrote the book, so that we could have a standard to judge it by. We wanted an intelligent adult with little or no technical background. We both chose our mothers. This is our way of saying "Thanks, Mom, for helping with this project and lots of others you didn't know about either."

Contents

CHAPTER 1

Computers Aren't Scary Anymore

By the time you finish reading this page, you will be able to do something that 95 percent of the people on this planet can't do. You will be able to write a simple program, load it into a computer and run it. By the time you finish reading this book you should know enough about computers to select one that is appropriate for your needs, and you'll know which of your needs a computer can fulfill. We hope this book will entertain, amuse, and enlighten you about small computers.

Not so sure you'll be able to program a computer by the end of the page? Have faith. Let's look at a simple program you can run on most small computers:

```
10 PRINT"HELLO, WHAT IS YOUR NAME?"
20 DIM N$(6)
30 INPUT N$
40 PRINT"WELL,",N$,"I'M GLAD YOU'VE COME
   OVER. I WAS LONELY."
```

Have your computer dealer show you how to *load* BASIC and turn the computer on. Then, load the program by typing it on the keyboard. Type it exactly as shown and press the RETURN key after each line. (Some computers will have a key labeled ENTER instead of RETURN.) Line 40 may go off the screen on the right side. Do not press RETURN until you have reached the end of the line.

Line 20 controls how long your name can be. If your name is longer than 6 letters, all of the letters from 7 on will be ignored. To change this, put a different number in the parentheses. After you have loaded in your program, type in RUN and press RETURN.

We agree that this silly little program doesn't really prove anything. Or does it? It has shown you that there is nothing frightening or magical about computers. That proves something. One of the biggest problems most people face in dealing with computers is fear. We've been taught to think of computers as big, complicated machines that, in the wrong hands, can do terrible things. We've been told for many years that the reason the bill was wrong was because the computer made a mistake. In reality, what happened was a human made a mistake and blamed it on the computer.

The computer is just like any other machine or tool. It is only as good as the person who runs it and only as useful as you make it. You can choose to use it in any manner you want. It won't take over your life, run off with your spouse, or cause you strife. It does only what you tell it to. If you don't want to learn anything beyond how to load a program into the machine and run it, you don't have to. You don't need to know how to program in *computer language*. There are thousands of *canned* programs available, covering a wide variety of subjects. Here are a few examples:

Educational Programs. Your grade-schooler can learn how to do fractions or you can learn how to read faster.

Personal Enrichment Programs. You can chart your biorhythms or play the stock market.

Game Programs. You can zap invaders from space with your laser ray or play chess.

Business Programs. You can manage yourself and your business better using word processing, spread-sheet analysis, investment analysis, or computerized accounting.

Arts Programs. You can paint abstract pictures on a video canvas or create the great American opera with a computer-controlled composing program.

These five areas as well as many others will be discussed in detail in the following chapters. Remember, a computer is a tool. How you use this fantastic tool is up to you. A computer has a lot of flexibility. It will do the same things a calculator will do (e.g., balance your checkbook), and it will do many more routine clerical jobs such as keeping track of Aunt Edna's birthday.

It will also do some very innovative jobs. For example, one of the most innovative programs we've heard about is one that keeps track of a three-year-old diabetic. It tells his parents when they should give him insulin, what his reaction to the insulin is, and how he is doing in general. The computer not only displays numerically his current vital signs, but also creates a graph which shows the trend across several days and weeks. The important thing about all of this is that the child's parents are just ordinary folks like you and me. Neither parent has any medical background or college training in computers. They taught themselves enough to create a modern miracle for their son. Take a minute to think about it. How could you use a computer to improve your life?

Perhaps you want to use a computer in your business. Thousands are doing it every day and the cost is less than you might think. It no longer costs $20,000 or more to buy a small business system. Some businesses actually do quite a bit of work with systems that cost less than $2,000. They won't keep track of ITT's cash flow, but they will do many jobs very nicely. You don't have to operate a small business to benefit from a computer; more managers buy computers than any other group.

O.K., so now you're interested. Where do we go from here? A good starting place is a local computer store or department store. A lot of places sell small computers today. When you visit a computer dealer you may have a communications problem. The salesperson may either know too much or too little, but don't become disheartened by this. We are going to tell you how to do the research on your own. This is exactly what you do when you buy a car or a microwave oven. Buying a computer is no different. There are very few people around who can tell you just what you need to know. It is quite possible to end up with a salesperson who knows less about computers than you do, especially where computers are a small and perhaps unimportant sideline. To an appliance or stereo salesperson, the computer may be just like another machine like a dishwasher, dryer, or range ("Yes ma'am, would you like one in coppertone or jungle green?"). In all fairness though, the salesperson may be the same kind of informed consumer you want to be. In fact, he or she may even own a computer. You'll just have to learn as much as you can and be prepared. You may even learn enough to deal with the people in a computer store.

The retail computer store was one of the most exciting new businesses of the seventies. You will meet real experts there. They may not, however, be able to talk to you on a level you

understand. Most computer stores were started by computer hobbyists—another word for "fanatic" when it comes to computers. Many such hobbyists can't understand why anyone would not want to learn everything there is to know about computers. To the devout there is no middle ground. If you like computers, you REALLY like them. It's hard for the hobbyists to understand that some people just want to use the computer as a tool, not adopt it into the family.

This is not to say that a computer store isn't a good place to buy a computer, because it is. Some of them just require you to make a little extra effort. The remainder of this book will help you deal with the problems of buying a computer. Be prepared, for instance, to experience some confusion when you go into a computer store. The technical jargon there may be wall-to-wall; terms like RAM and ROM, Pascal and BASIC, DOS and Disk may abound. You'll find out what the most important terms mean as you read this book, and we have included a glossary, so hang in there. In fact, we urge you to read this book all the way through before making that first serious computer buying safari (short sorties and patrols are O.K., though).

This book is organized so that you can skip around if you want to. In the next chapter, "101 Things You Can Do with Your Computer Right Now," we will introduce you to some *canned* programs.

Chapters 4, 5, 6, and 7 all end with a discussion of how to buy a computer for a specific application. Chapter 3, "How to Buy Your Own Computer," introduces the subject. It gives seven steps that will help you buy the right computer for you.

What can you do with a computer? You'll find some of the answers in Chapter 4, "The Home Computer." Here you'll see how you can use your computer for entertainment, personal development, personal finance, investment and taxes, hobbies, home control, and health.

One of the most exciting uses of a small computer is communication. In Chapter 5, "The Outer Limits: Communicating with the World," you will find out how you can tie into someone else's information base such as UPI, AP, or Dow Jones. You will be introduced to new ideas like electronic mail, networks, teleconferencing, and information management.

If you are interested in education, you will want to read Chapter 6, "The Teaching Machine." Here you will see how the computer can help you learn things or teach your children. If you are a teacher, you will find some ideas for using a computer in your classroom.

Can you use a computer in your business? You'll find the answer to this question in Chapter 7, "The Working Computer." In this chapter you'll find out how managers use computers, and we'll talk about how computers can be used in a small business.

A computer is nothing more than a box of parts until someone tells it what to do. Chapter 8, "The Stuff That Makes It Happen: Software," will help you understand how to talk to a computer.

You don't have to know anything about automotive mechanics to drive your car and you don't have to know anything about computer electronics to operate a computer. But, if you would like to know a little bit about computer electronics, you will want to read Chapter 9, "It's Not Magic: The Basic Computer." This chapter presents a brief overview of a typical computer system. You'll find out why your air conditioner might cause your computer problems and what you can do about it.

Chapter 10, "The Current Crop," is a survey of most of the currently available small computers. We have limited our discussion to popular computers but this chapter will give you a starting point.

If you want to play music, communicate with the world, or print things out, you will need *peripherals*. In Chapter 11, "Computer Peripherals," we'll describe most of the things you might need or want.

In every chapter, we have given you the titles of a few books that you might want to read. In addition, we have surveyed book and magazine publishers in Chapter 12, "Where to Find Everything We Didn't Tell You."

The personal computer is one of the most exciting inventions in all of history. It gives you the opportunity to interact with the world around you in ways that weren't possible five years ago, and new applications are being introduced almost daily.

Before you go blazing off into your favorite chapter, though, we'd like to tell you that neither of us has a university degree in computer science (Jerry has a Ph.D. in clinical psychology, Merl has a degree in engineering). Both of us use computers extensively in our professional lives and in our homes, however. We hope that *Computers for Everybody* will be your first step in becoming an enthusiastic computer user too.

With that in mind, you might be interested in how computers came about. This section won't help you buy or use your computer, but we hope you will find it interesting.

"Since the turn of the century, only a handful of significant developments have directly affected the everyday lives of all of us—the electric light bulb, telephone, automobile, radio, television and most recently, the electronic digital computer, whose impact may be the most encompassing and dramatic of all." This comment sums it up. It is the introductory sentence from Herman Lukoff's *From Dits to Bits...A Personal History of the Electronic Computer* (dilithium Press). If you are interested in the development of the modern-day computer you may want to read Mr. Lukoff's book. It deals with the development of the first electronic digital computer at the University of Pennsylvania. Another book, *The Making of the Micro* by Christopher Evans (Van Nostrand Reinhold), will also be of interest to the reader who wants more detail on the history of computers. *The Making of the Micro* begins several hundred years before the development of the first electronic computer and describes the concepts, theories, and inventions that led to the development of modern computers. In this chapter, we will limit our sketch of computer history to only the most recent developments.

One of the first fully functioning electronic computers was developed at the University of Pennsylvania during World War II. The initial idea was to develop a device that could both determine missile trajectories and predict the weather. Within a few years, however, the machine was being used for a variety of business and government applications. By 1952, it was predicting election outcomes, and a company called International Business Machines had entered the field in a big way.

We don't need to tell you the effect IBM had on the beginning computer business, but we are getting ahead of ourselves. A lot of things helped bring about the first modern personal computer. The first was the transistor.

The invention of the transistor in 1948 made modern computers practical because of the transistor's dependability, small size, and low power requirements. Transistors quickly replaced vacuum tubes as the building blocks of computers, and the computer age was underway. Since then several major advances in semiconductor technology have produced smaller and smaller components that do more and more work.

In the late 1950s and early 60s the *integrated circuit* or *IC* was developed. An IC contains several transistors, resistors, and capacitors in a circuit that is enclosed in a single small case. Large Scale Integrated (LSI) circuits followed soon afterward with hundreds, then thousands of components packed into a single chip. It may be somewhat misleading to say that there are *components* inside an IC. Actually there is generally one chip of material such as silicon on which several different layers of other types of material have been deposited. The pattern of these layers creates the effect of transistors, resistors, and capacitors without the necessity of manufacturing individual components and then installing them in a circuit.

In 1970, a new type of IC, the *microprocessor*, was produced. This *computer on a chip* is what makes personal computers possible. A single chip today contains the same amount of computing power that took tons of equipment thirty years ago. One early computer, ENIAC, occupied 3,000 cubic feet of space, used 140,000 watts of power, weighed 30 tons, and had 18,000 tubes, 70,000 resistors, and 10,000 capacitors. Today the VIC microcomputer from Commodore weighs about four pounds and uses only a few watts of power. Yet it is more powerful than ENIAC and does its work much faster. The VIC is also about 10,000 times more reliable and costs less than a good set of snow tires.

Since the fifties, computers have steadily become smaller and cheaper, and this pattern has produced a change in the types of people who use them. Early computers were within the financial reach of only a few large companies, universities, and government agencies. But as the price decreased, com-

ENIAC

puters became more cost-effective for more and more companies, especially those with large amounts of routine numerical operations to be done. Almost every bank today, for example, uses a computer to maintain accounts. The large, fill-up-the-room computers that large businesses use are called *mainframe* computers.

As the technology of producing semiconductor integrated circuits advanced, a new type of computer—the minicomputer—emerged. Instead of occupying entire rooms like the giant mainframes from IBM, the mini is more the size of a large color television. Digital Equipment Corporation sold thousands of their PDP-8 minicomputers to businesses that did not need a larger computer. Steel fabricators, for example, developed programs for the PDP-8 that allowed them to precisely control the steel-fabricating process by computer. Scientists used minis to control experiments in the laboratory without tying up a large computer, and trucking companies

DEC PDP-8

used them to arrange routings, to compute charges, and to do paperwork.

The minicomputer brought the power of the computer to small businesses, but not to individuals. Although the cost of a mini has dropped considerably in the past few years, a typical business system still costs over $20,000, much more than the average individual can afford.

An honest-to-goodness computer revolution occurred in 1971, however, when Intel Corporation produced the first microprocessor or *computer on a chip*, the 4004. It was a crude, expensive device that was used primarily in commercial settings. In 1972, Intel produced the 8080, a more sophisticated microprocessor that was cheap enough to be attractive to individuals interested in computers. Its use was limited, however, by a shortage of the support chips needed to create a working 8080 computer system, and by the fact that few people knew exactly what to do with a computer on a chip. Intel marketed the 8080 chip in 1973, and it became the foundation for a

whole new industry—personal computing. Although it cost several hundred dollars in 1974 and was hard to find, the 8080 can be ordered by mail today for well under $10. Its position of preeminence, however, has been lost. Newer, more powerful chips such as the Zilog Z80, the Intel 8088, the Intel 8086, and the Motorola 68000 are used in many of the newer models of small computers. At the beginning of 1983 no popular computer used the 8080. It was, however, the chip that got things started.

At about the same time Intel was busy creating computer integrated circuits, another important ingredient in the personal computing movement was emerging. Hardware, the actual computer and its accessories, is only half of a computer system. To get it to do anything useful the computer must be given a set of instructions that tell it exactly what to do. These instructions are called *programs* or *software*, and they are at least as important as the nuts and bolts of a system.

Until the early seventies not many programs existed that would be of interest to the individual computer user. Few of us, for example, need to know where a 60mm shell would land if fired from a particular artillery piece at a 30 degree angle in a ten-mile-an-hour crosswind, nor do we have a use for a program that will calculate the load capacity of a 30-foot steel beam. In the early days of computing the instructions (or software) were written in a way that was easy for computers to understand but not so easy for people. Programming a computer was thus a specialized task that required sophisticated training. In 1963, however, a simple computer language called BASIC, Beginners All-purpose Symbolic Instruction Code, was developed by John Kemeny and Thomas Kurtz at Dartmouth College. BASIC is easy to learn, yet is a powerful way of talking to the computer in a language that is similar to English.

The creation of BASIC made computers easily accessible to thousands of people who had no previous contact with them. People like Bob Albrecht, then with Digital Equipment Corporation (DEC), spread the gospel of BASIC through workshops, introductory books and general enthusiasm. David Ahl, another DEC employee, was also a preacher of the BASIC gospel. Between them Ahl and Albrecht helped to create a collection of recreational programs written in BASIC that made computers available, and interesting, to thousands. Believers then taught others how to use minicomputers to play games, draw pictures, and provide instruction. Albrecht, Ahl, and their followers are still in the forefront of the personal computing movement. The People's Computer Company, a nonprofit group founded by Albrecht, now publishes several magazines for the individual interested in computers. Ahl founded *Creative Computing*, a popular magazine, and published *101 BASIC Computer Games*. The book first appeared in 1973. It is still available and highly recommended for those who are even slightly interested in the recreational side of computers.

Although Ahl and Albrecht were excited about the personal computing market, their employer, DEC, had about as much as it could handle from its traditional customers (e.g., small businesses, universities, government agencies) and made little effort to move into the new field. DEC's support for BASIC, however, and its encouragement of the development of recreational uses of minicomputers helped create a small army of informed consumers who wanted more—and at a price they could afford.

In 1974, that market was tapped. Several companies offered computer kits that could be assembled by users. All used microprocessor chips such as the 8080. The result was an inexpensive *microcomputer* system that, at least theoretically, would do many of the things a PDP-8 minicomputer would do. By taking advantage of technological advances in large scale integration these companies were able to build a working computer that was about the same size as a home stereo system. The best known of these early kits was the Mark-8 which used an Intel 8080 microprocessor chip. Over 1200 people ordered the Mark-8 kit after it was described in a 1974 *Popular Electronics* article. The kits offered during that time were financial failures. Assembling and operating one of these early kits still required a fair level of sophistication in electronics and computer logic to make them work. These qualifications severely limited the market for the first microprocessor kits. They were, however, the leading edge.

The market and product both changed in late 1974 when an obscure company with the unlikely name of Micro Instrumentation and Telemetry (MITS) produced its first microcomputer. MITS was founded in 1969 by H. Edward Roberts to produce electronic systems for model rockets. With about $10,000 in equipment and a $400 investment from four partners, Roberts moved from model rockets to calculators and began selling a low-cost programmable calculator in 1971 for $199. Comparable units from Hewlett Packard cost thousands. Their success in the calculator market led MITS into the hand-held calculator field at a time when giants like Texas Instruments were about to settle down to a serious price war. MITS was an early casualty in that war and borrowed heavily to avoid closing down permanently. Roberts decided his next venture would be in the personal computing market, and in 1974 a MITS microcomputer kit was featured on the cover of *Popular Electronics*. Named Altair by Roberts' daughter (after a planet in a "Star Trek" episode), the kit was an instant success. MITS expected 800 orders in 1975; they shipped 1500 units in the first two months at $398 each.

The Altair was the first commercially successful microcomputer, but as demand for it increased, the time between placing an order and receiving the kit also increased. These long delays at MITS created a place for several other companies like IMSAI, Southwest Technical Products Corporation, Processor Technology, and Digital Group. Between 1975 and 1977, these companies also began offering microcomputers and accessories to a market which grew to include people from nearly all walks of life. Competition since 1974 has been tough and, with the exception of Southwest, all of these pioneering companies are gone now. One problem that plagued most, if not all, the early microcomputer manufacturers was reliability. Many produced equipment that never worked properly and almost all sold at least a few models that had such serious problems that regular, dependable operation was unlikely. Another problem was the lack of software for the machines. These microcomputers were often purchased by individuals who planned to do their own programming. Those who bought the computers expecting to be able to buy many programs that allowed them to use the computer for business or professional applications were often disappointed. The lack of good quality software was a major problem.

Although some people have referred to microcomputers and their use by individuals as a *hobby*, the fact is that most people who buy a micro have some idea in the back of their head about using it in their profession, business, schoolwork, or in some consumer-related project. We prefer to use the term *personal computing* rather than hobby computing in referring to use of micros by individuals. Personal computing is the use of a small computer by an individual, small group, or family for recreational, business, or other personal purposes.

The computers offered by MITS, Processor Technology and others can be considered second-generation machines with the Mark-8 being first generation. The Altair and its competitors generally were available in assembled as well as kit form, had BASIC as a standard language, and could be attached to a variety of accessories (e.g., printers, televisions) with only a few technical adaptations. These second-generation machines were still being refined and improved when a third generation emerged. During 1977 and 1978, several companies brought mass merchandising to personal computing. Radio Shack, Commodore, and Apple Computer Company all offered third generation computers designed specifically for the beginner in

Commodore PET

personal computing who had neither the electronics background nor the knowledge of computers that characterized many of those who bought second-generation systems. These computers all come assembled and have been designed so that all you have to do is unpack the system, plug it in, and begin operating immediately.

BASIC is usually *built-in* so that you can use English-like words to talk to the computer. The third generation computer is more reliable than second generation systems and there is generally a large amount of software available. Third generation systems tend to be more self-contained as well. That is, you do not have to build any of the components required to make them work, and you do not have to buy parts from several different sources to assemble a complete system.

Third generation computers are still on the market. The Apple II, in fact, is one of the best selling computers currently in production while Commodore and Radio Shack have retired their early models and now offer several new systems with a variety of features.

What has happened to the market since 1977-78? Quite a bit. Current models offer sophisticated features such as sound synthesis, voice synthesis (the computer talks) and voice recognition (the computer listens to you), remarkable color graphics, simpler operating characteristics, greater capacities, and lower costs for equivalent features. In addition, the personal computer field now has an increasing number of *big name* manufacturers, such as IBM, DEC, Xerox, Atari, Sony, Hitachi, Toshiba, and Canon. Although some people predicted the demise of early second generation computer producers such as Apple and Radio Shack when IBM and the Japanese entered the market, such has not been the case. The small computer field is expanding so rapidly that successful products from new entrants such as IBM have not kept new models from older (though smaller) small computer manufacturers from selling briskly.

Software has also become an important computer *feature* for today's buyers. Six years ago a company could market a machine and promise the buying public that software was *in the works*. Today, a computer without a large collection of available software is destined for failure, and few manufacturers would even consider bringing out a new model without plenty of software.

Today there is some indication that the market is beginning to specialize. Most third generation computers tried to be all things to all people. The same computer was sold as a great home system, perfect for the office, just the thing for an active professional who needed his or her own computer, and the best educational computer on the market. Although many new models are still designed and sold as general purpose small computers, a number of others are clearly aimed at one segment of the market.

The NorthStar Advantage and the Eagle computer, for example, are clearly intended for the business market. Their design, their standard features, and the software available for them all support the business market well. The Commodore Vic, on the other hand, is clearly a home computer with recreational and computer literacy goals in mind. Its low price and the availability of many recreational programs make it likely to be seen almost exclusively in the home.

Sharp and Panasonic both offer several models of hand-held computers that meet the needs of construction engineers and real estate agents for a portable computer that can perform on-the-spot calculations without the necessity of being in the office. In a similar vein, the Osborne I and the Kaypro II computers are portable systems which can be carried like a briefcase (a rather heavy briefcase, that is). Professionals who need a computer while on the road are buying these by the thousands. One reporter even took an Osborne I into Afghanistan and wrote his stories on it while traveling with the rebel forces. Using a rechargeable battery pack, he was able to use it virtually anywhere. When he returned to Pakistan he connected the computer to a telephone and transmitted the stories back to the U.S.

In the coming years we are likely to see more models designed for specific segments of the small computer market.

CHAPTER 2

Things You Can Do with Your Computer Right Now

A computer is only a dumb box with a bunch of electronic things in it. All the talk about all the marvelous things computers can do is really only talk about all the marvelous things software can do. In this chapter, we will show you some of the things you can do with your computer. We will describe a few (101) computer programs, or software. There are literally thousands of programs available for nearly every computer on the market so our list is somewhat selective. These are real programs, not hypothetical ideas about what computers can do. They are produced by reputable companies and are all available right now. A listing in this chapter is by no means an endorsement. All we have tried to do is give you a sampling of what is available.

The programs are separated into four major areas: Personal, Educational, Business, and Professional and Managerial. We will explain each area as we go. The purpose of this chapter is to give you a feel for what kinds of things you can do with your computer. Therefore, we suggest that you read all of the descriptions. Publishers' addresses are shown in Appendix A.

All of these publishers will be more than willing to send you a complete description and pricing information for their programs. You might also want to check out the store where you bought this book.

PERSONAL

Programs in this section are intended for home use. We'll start with games because games can be both entertaining and educational. Since your "home computer" can do more than play games we have included a wide variety of other things. For instance, you can count calories, invest in the stock market, write poetry, or learn how to speed read.

Apple Panic—You have probably eaten a few apples in your life. Now, it's their turn. In this game, all sorts of things attack you: apples, mobile fruit, butterflies and other sorts of monsters you thought were harmless. *Broderbund Software*

Groan—If you love games but hate computers then you will enjoy *Groan*. This simple dice game will both frustrate and delight you. You play against the computer and try to outscore it. You get one turn then the computer gets a turn. The dice have five of the same six numbers that other dice have. However, the one is replaced by a groan face. If you get a groan on your turn, you lose all of the points you have accumulated on that turn. If you get two groans you lose everything. The computer can have the same bad luck that you do. *dilithium Software*

Management Simulator—This program is both an excellent teaching tool and an intellectual game. Each player controls a company that manufactures three products. The winner is the player who has the highest stock price at the end of the game. *Dynacomp*

Star Raiders—You are the pilot of a starcraft. Your mission is to save the galaxy from the Zylons. This exciting game can be played at five different skill levels. At each level the game becomes more difficult and the Zylons become more dangerous. *Atari*

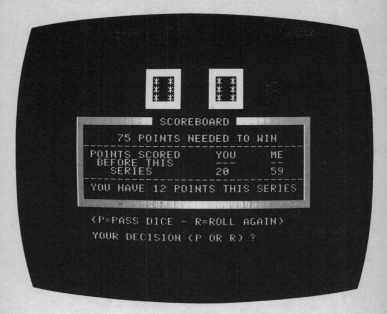

GROAN

Lunar Lander—Now that you are in orbit over the moon, you must land. This game takes both skill and practice. *Interactive Microware*

Sunmax—This educational solar game challenges you to guess the correct angle for fixed, flat-plate solar collectors. It is both educational and fun. *Solartek*

Eastern Front—Like any really good game, Eastern Front is easy to play but difficult, if not impossible, to master. It is a World War II simulation. In this game you are a German general in charge of invading Russia in 1941. *Atari*

Sargon: A Computer Chess Program—You can play with either black or white, and you can play against the computer or set up problems and watch the computer solve them. In either case, the computer puts a chess board on the video display, and, as moves are made, the board on the screen changes. *Hayden*

Three Mile Island—This program is a realistic simulation of a pressurized nuclear reactor. You can learn how to operate a reactor and study safety factors. *Muse Software*

Crossword Magic

Crossword Magic—Have you ever wanted to design crossword puzzles? This is your chance. All you have to do is supply the words and the program designs the puzzle. *L & S Computerware*

Market—In this two-player game you are president of a company that manufactures racing bicycles; so is your opponent. The program sets up all production and variable costs. It then assigns initial values for inventory, cash on hand and total assets. You must make marketing decisions. At the end of each quarter the program tells you how you have done. *Creative Computing Software*

Deadline—You are about to investigate one of the deadliest plots in the annals of crime. This is a game designed for murder mystery fans and natural problem solvers. Can you find the murderer before the 12-hour deadline? *Infocom*

Electric Duet—This music synthesizer lets you create or play music. It has its own music library. Your computer can play two notes at the same time. *Insoft*

Graph It—This program will let you draw one, two, and three dimension graphs. You can plot curves, lines and equations. *Atari*

Microcomputer Flight Simulator—This is not a game. This realistic simulation lets you take off, fly, navigate, and land an airplane. *Dynacomp*

Kaleido—In the color section of this book you will see a typical pattern generated by *Kaleido*. This program creates a series of kaleidoscope-like designs with each one overlapping the previous one. *dilithium Software*

Haiku—A computer is just a number cruncher. Right? Wrong! With this program, you can use the computer to write Japanese Haiku poetry. *Technical Products Company*

Slide Show—This program generates a series of digitized color pictures on your display. *Apple*

McTerm—Now you can communicate with the world. With the McTerm software and a modem you can turn your computer into an intelligent terminal. You can interact with large and small computers anywhere in the word. *Madison Computer*

Data Analysis—This program calculates the mean, standard error of a single observation, and error of the mean of a set of data. It also does curve fitting. *Data Analysis*

Pearl—If you would like to develop your own programs but you don't know how, this may be the answer. To write a program with *Pearl* you use the screen like a piece of paper in a typewriter. *Pearl* does the rest. *Relational Systems*

Color Calendar—Got a busy schedule? You can organize it with this program. With the daily schedule you can review any day of the month and schedule an event or activity. *Spectrum Software*

Graphics Tablet—This device lets you draw and animate characters on your computer screen. Everything is shown in brilliant color. *Apple*

Softside—*Softside* is not a program. It is, however, one of the most innovative new ideas since the computer. *Softside* is a magazine that is published in both standard and electronic formats. In other words, there is both a paper version and a disk version. You receive both of them each month. There are at least four usable programs per issue. *Softside*

Micro-Deutsch—Have you always wanted to learn German? Here's your chance. The 24 grammar lessons use substitution transformation drills, item ordering, translations and verb drills. *Krell Software*

SpeedRead—This speed reading tutor begins with training your eyes and mind to function together. It trains you to recognize phrases and columns and it exercises your peripheral vision. *Optimized Systems Software*

Checkbook—This program takes you through the necessary steps to balance your checkbook. It starts off by giving you instructions about how to verify that the amount of each check and each deposit are the same on the statement as they are in

your checkbook. Then it asks for the ending balance shown on the bank statement. It continues to ask questions until you have entered sufficient information to balance your checkbook. *Creative Software*

Star-Pak—Are you an amateur astronomer? This program computes Julian Dates, Sidereal time, days-of-week, sunrise/sunset, moonrise/moonset, precession and coordinate transformations. *ATMCO*

Personal Computer Home Management System—This is a system that keeps track of names, medical records, insurance policies, credit cards and anything else you want. It also has a 20-year calendar, metric conversion, an alarm timer, and a display of the time in other parts of the world. *Arlington Software Systems*

EDUCATIONAL PROGRAMS

Although small computers are not in a majority of schoolrooms today, they are appearing in schools in increasing numbers, where they are used to teach everything from reading readiness to advanced mathematics. Small computers are also being purchased by parents who want to provide their children with computer-based educational experiences at home. Here are a few of the educational programs available today.

College Board—This set of programs provides high school students with training designed to help them improve their scores on college entrance examinations. *Krell Software*

Sensational Simulations—These programs provide students with a simulated experience in an interesting environment. You may be the ruler of an ancient kingdom whose decisions will determine whether the country prospers and grows or declines and falls. Or you may be a fur trader in colonial times who must make decisions that mean life and death for your trading party in hostile territory. If something more modern is called for, you can be a stock broker trying to make your fortune in a simulated stock market. *Creative Computing Software*

Milliken Math Sequences—This comprehensive package of programs provides students with practice on the math skills taught in grades 1 through 8. It keeps track of each student's assignments as well as performance. It does diagnostic testing, and can be used with as many as 500 students. *Milliken*

Map Reading—*Map Reading* teaches basic map reading skills using the color graphics features of the Apple II computer. Useful with fourth graders through adult. *Micro Power and Light Company*

Early Learning Fun—This program uses color graphics and sound on the Texas Instruments computer to teach preschool children shape, number, and letter recognition as well as counting, sorting, and the alphabet. *Texas Instruments*

Physics Compulab—This series of programs enables the Apple II computer to simulate a large number of physics experiments. Students using the programs make measurements of simulated events created by the computer just as they would do if conducting a real experiment. The programs cover simulations in statistics, parabolic motion, nonconstant acceleration, planetary motion, wave motion, and electric fields. *EduTech*

Punctuation—There are two programs in this series. They

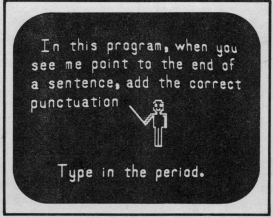

Punctuation

use color graphics, animation, and sound to teach children how to use the period, question mark, exclamation point, and comma.
Educational Activities

Logo—Available from several different companies, this is not a specific applications program. It is a language with features particularly well-suited to giving young children their first computer experience while helping them develop more sophisticated thinking skills.

Early Reading—Another program from Texas Instruments that teaches children some of the basic skills required in early reading. The program costs $55 but requires an optional speech synthesizer before it can be used. The computer "talks" to the child who can respond by pressing keys on the keyboard. *Texas Instruments*

Pilot—This is another language which is useful in educational settings. There are versions of PILOT for virtually every small computer on the market today. Most versions are designed for use by teachers who want to develop their own computer-assisted learning lessons. Some versions, such as Atari PILOT, are designed for use by teachers and for use as a first language for students who work with computers in their classrooms or at home. Prices for PILOT range from $20 to $200. Quality also varies but does not necessarily coincide with price.

Arcademic Skill Builders—Produced by an established educational publisher, this series of programs uses color graphics and arcade-like games to teach basic skills. One program, for example, requires you to protect your planet from a series of deadly invaders who are dropping from the sky. Instead of zapping them with your laser ray, however, you must solve the math problem that appears on the side of each of the alien ships. Titles in this series include Alien Addition, Minus Mission, Meteor Multiplication, Demolition Division, Alligator Mix, and Dragon Mix. There may not be a more enjoyable way to learn your basic math skills. Available from *Developmental Learning Materials*.

Music Maker—This program helps the user create computer music. It displays a music staff on the screen and accepts input from the keyboard. Once the piece of music has been input it can be "played" by the computer or saved on tape or diskette for use later. Cost is around $40. Available from Texas Instruments for the TI computer. A similar program is available for the ATARI computers.

Music Skills Trainer—This program drills students in pitch recognition, interval recognition, chord recognition, and musical phrase recall. *Texas Instruments*

Social Studies, Elementary Volume 3—This set of programs is one of several which were developed by the Minnesota Educational Computer Consortium. There are six simulations which will run on the Apple or Atari computers. One simulation, Civil War, simulates 14 of the major battles in the Civil War. One student (or group of students) takes the role of commander of the Confederate forces while another takes the role of the Union commander. The decisions the students make determine the outcome of the battles.

Sell Lemonade—*Sell Lemonade* is a simulation that teaches students to run a small business efficiently even in the face of problems such as thunderstorms, heat waves, and street construction. *Creative Computing*

Clock—*Clock* teaches children to read time from a standard clock. It makes use of the PET graphics and animation features. *Scholastic*

Energy Czar—You are the Energy Czar of the United States. If you are to stave off a total collapse of the nation you must reduce energy demands, find new sources, and manage to keep your job by keeping the public opinion polls from getting so negative that you are fired. The simulation requires you to decide in the beginning whether your policies will be pro-fossil, pro-nuclear, or pro-solar. If you are successful and get a national public opinion poll rating of 75 percent or higher, you become a national hero. *Atari*

Mastertype—This is a drill program for touch typing. Drill, however, usually conjures up an image of something dull and boring. Not with *Mastertype*. Students are presented with a colorful graphic display with their home key location in the middle of the screen. From four corners of the screen menacing missiles move toward home base. Each missile has a word or letter sequence associated with it. If you type that word correctly, the missile is destroyed. If you don't type it correctly before it gets to the center of the screen, civilization as we know it is destroyed. The program adjusts its speed as the student improves. One of the best programs of its type (pun intended). It has over thirty standard sets of words which students can practice plus the ability to accept custom word lists you create. *Mastertype*

Chemistry Lab Simulations #1—This is one of the better science simulations. The simulations make extensive use of color graphics. They cover introductory chemistry lab experiments in a number of areas (e.g., acid based titration experiment, a pH-meter experiment, a monomolecular film experiment). *High Technology, Inc.*

BUSINESS

The programs listed in this section are intended primarily for small businesses. You probably already know that a computer can help you with your accounting. But, did you know that it can also help you get a loan, spell things correctly, and plan your future? It will do all these things and more.

```
        PARTS INVENTORY PROGRAM  PAR        DATE 11-28-00

                   TABLE OF OPERATIONS

    A = ADD PART NUMBER                Q = QUICK REGISTER

    C = CHANGE THE PARTS FILE DATA     R = REPORTS

    D = ENTER DATE                     S = SORT

    F = FIND PARTS STATUS              T = TURNOVER

    L = LIST THE INVENTORY             V = VENDOR FILE

    N = NO (LOST) SALE                 X = INDEX PARTS FILE

    O = ORDER PARTS                    Z = SWAP DATA DISKS.

    P = POST SALES AND ARRIVALS        END = END PROGRAM


SELECT ACTION FROM TABLE ABOVE ▮
```

Parts Inventory Program

General Ledger—CMS Software publishes a comprehensive accounting package that may suit your needs. The general ledger package maintains account balances for the present month, the quarter to date, and the year to date. Appropriate entries are automatically posted to the cash disbursements journal, the cash receipts journal, and the general journal. *CMS Software*

Accounts Receivable—The CMS A/R package prepares invoices and monthly statements. Invoices may be distributed among nine different GL accounts with automatic updating to the general ledger. *CMS Software*

Accounts Payable—This program prepares checks with full voucher detail. Invoices may be distributed among nine different GL accounts with automatic updating. *CMS Software*

Payroll—Like the other CMS programs, the payroll program automatically updates the general ledger. It prepares checks with full deductions and pay detail and it can be used for weekly, biweekly, semi-monthly, or monthly employees. *CMS Software*

DataStar—*DataStar* is a data handling program that allows you to enter, retrieve, and update data without creating special forms. It can be used as the data entry portion for inventory, accounting, or other application programs. *MicroPro*

AMWAY Product Distributor Programs—Perhaps you think your business is too small or too specialized to benefit from a computer. Here are a group of programs that help any AMWAY distributor. These programs generate and check orders, track distributors, and do basic bookkeeping. *Blechman Enterprises*

Loan—One of the most frustrating things about borrowing money is that it is difficult to evaluate all your options. With this program, you can vary information any way you want and make an intelligent decision based on this information. *dilithium Software*

Manufacturing Software Package—This system is designed for companies that gross between $5 million and $100 million. It allows you to coordinate and control the following functions: stock room, work in progress, finished goods in inventory, job and product cost accounting, labor distribution, purchasing, and product structure maintenance. *Mercator Business Systems*

```
67500 FOR 360 MONTHS AT 11.75 PER CENT
          REMAINING    -----INTEREST-----
MONTH     BALANCE      MONTH      TO-DATE
1         67479.58     660.94     660.94
2         67458.96     660.74     1321.68
3         67438.14     660.54     1982.22
4         67417.11     660.33     2642.55
5         67395.88     660.13     3302.68
6         67374.44     659.92     3962.60
7         67352.79     659.71     4622.31
8         67330.93     659.50     5281.81
9         67308.85     659.28     5941.09
10        67286.56     659.07     6600.16
11        67264.05     658.85     7259.01
12        67241.32     658.63     7917.64
13        67218.36     658.40     8576.04
14        67195.18     658.18     9234.22
15        67171.77     657.95     9892.17
16        67148.13     657.72     10549.89

PRESS 'T' FOR TOTALS, OR
ANY OTHER KEY FOR NEXT SCREEN
```

Loan

Shorttax—This income planning program computes income and social security taxes of individuals, trusts, and corporations for six tax years. It can determine regular income tax, tax using income averaging, 50 percent maximum tax on earned income, add-on minimum tax, and alternative minimum tax. *Syntax*

Busicomp—This is a completely integrated interactive business system designed to handle the accounting needs of a small business. All of the standard journals and ledgers are provided. Busicomp generates 41 different reports. *Advanced Operating Systems*

Microaccountant—This general purpose financial accounting system gives you a standard double entry ledger system.

09:37:17 AM   Cyber-Farmer 80 Options Menu   10/01/82
RESTART CYBER-FARMER 80
BEFORE CHANGING DATA DISKS

1) Journal Entries   2) Journal-Ledger Update
3) Cash Flow   4) Budget
5) Depreciation   6) Inventory
7) Disk Backup   8) Paper Advance
9) Account Maintenance   10) General Information Review
11) Disk Reorganization   12) Change date and time
13) Exit to Basic

Choose Option by Number [   ]

Cyber-Farmer

You can have up to 300 accounts in the general ledger. A report generator will prepare transaction journal listings, individual account transactions and balances, net income statements, etc. *Spectrum Software*

Qsort—This program sorts lists based on your alphabetic or numeric data into ascending or descending order. *Structured Systems Group*

Cyber–Farmer—This is a complete farm accounting package. It records, sorts, combines and prints the results of the farm operation. It keeps personal, family, and household accounts as well. *Cyberia*

Bookkeeper I—This simple to use system was developed for very small businesses. You don't have to know anything about computers, software or accounting to be able to use it. *Data Train, Inc.*

Tax Planning Program—This program is designed for a small accounting practice. The program estimates taxes for individuals and corporations. It uses such variables as personal service income, capital gains, rents, dividends, and ordinary corportate income. *Charles Mann and Associates*

Business Planner—This program will help you start your own business. Business Planner prepares a model that can continue working for you. It will help you provide the financial proof you need to fund your business. *Duosoft*

PROFESSIONAL AND MANAGERIAL

The manager's desktop computer may be the most powerful managerial tool ever developed. It is certainly the most versatile. With a small computer sitting on your desk, you can process words, unscramble numbers, and talk to Dow Jones.

1–2–3—is an *integrated* software product. It combines an electronic spread sheet with database management, graphics, and limited word processing. The spread sheet alone is reason enough to buy this product. It has capabilities far beyond those found in older spreadsheets such as VisiCalc and SuperCalc. *Lotus*

VisiCalc—Thousands of managers feel that *VisiCalc* alone is reason enough to buy a computer. This extremely popular program lets you create an electronic spread sheet. The spread sheet has more uses than even the program developers imagined, but here are a few: financial analysis, sales projections, expense accounts, and portfolio management. *VisiCorp*

A Sample output from VisiCalc

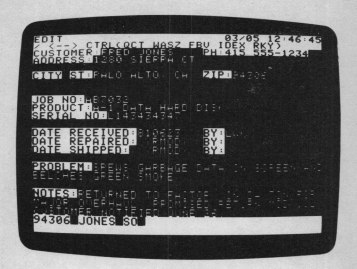

VisiDex

Wordstar—*Wordstar* is a screen-oriented word processing system. The screen shows you exactly what will be printed, so the program is relatively easy to use. It can be used with a variety of other Micropro programs that will automatically address letters, compute table information, and correct your spelling. *Micropro*

VisiDex—This program is a tie-in to *VisiCalc*. The VisiDex program operates like a giant set of cross referenced index cards. Each card can be stored and recalled later. Cards can be cross referenced by key words or dates. *VisiCorp*

SuperCalc—This program is an improvement on *VisiCalc* in many ways. It offers many of the same functions plus some enhancements that *VisiCalc* does not have. *Sorcim*

MBA—This program combines a spread sheet analysis program, a data base management program and a word processor. (If you are unsure what these terms mean, here are some examples: *VisiCalc* is a spread sheet analysis program, *Microbook* is a data base management program and *Executive Assistant* is a word processing program.) This program should save a lot of time in report generation. It has all of the essential elements of any report built in. *Context Management Systems*

32 VisiCalc Worksheets—This program is a tie-in to *VisiCalc* that will help you get started. Thirty-two of the most common applications have been outlined. All you need to do is enter the data. *dilithium Software*

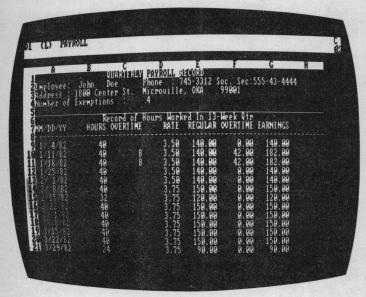

A VisiCalc Worksheet

Job Costing—You can maintain as much or as little job information as you want with this program. It is completely independent of the general ledger but it can be integrated. *Arkansas Systems, Inc.*

Proforma—What is your cash flow going to be like for the next 12 months or next 12 quarters? *Proforma* will help you project cash flow for each of twelve periods. *Management Systems Software*

Milestone—Here is your chance to increase your productivity by taking advantage of the latest developments in computer technology. If you are familiar with the critical-path-analysis method of analysis, then you know how useful this program can be. It lets you divide a large project into a group of manageable smaller projects. *Digital Marketing*

```
PROJECT SCHEDULE        Keys are ===/critical,:::/done,—/normal,.../slack
                         Jan                    Feb              Mar
Revision 9, 3/16/81      1   8  15  22  29   5  12  19  26   5  12
Job (Room for 121 more)  0   1   2   3   4   5   6   7   8   9  10
 1 Purchase the pipe     >————)...)
 2 Dig 1st part of tren  >————)...)
 3 Purchase fittings     >===========)
 4 Lay 1st part of pipe            >=======)
 5 Dig 2nd part of trench      >——)  )
 6 Fill 1st part of trench         >——)  )
 7 Lay 2nd part of pipe            >======)
 8 Fill 2nd part of trench             >===)
 9 Repave street                           >========)
10 Repair sidewalk                     >——)       )
11 Project completed                              %


   Manpower level=4    4   4   6   6   9   6   4   3   3   0
   Direct cost in K$=75 0   5  13   8  10   5  10  30   0   0
A(dd E(rase or I(nsert a job       move U(p D(own L(eft R(ight or H(ome
M(odify or C(omplete a job             O(ther options              Q(uit
To select an option, press its letter; numbers can prefix a move _
```

Milestone

TeloFacts—is a questionnaire evaluation and analysis program. It can be used to create and evaluate any kind of questionnaire, e.g. tests, job applications, market surveys, etc. It will present the results by score, rank, or a variety of other correlations. *dilithium Software*

Dow Jones Series Portfolio Evaluator—With this program, you can store, modify, and update approximately 100 individual portfolios of up to 50 stocks. In addition, the program includes a terminal program that lets you access the Dow Jones News/Retrieval System. *Apple*

The Personal Investor—Consistently making money in the stock market requires time-consuming hard work. This package consists of three programs that give you the facts you need. The *News/Terminal* program automatically connects your computer to the Dow Jones News/Retrieval Service. *Stock Portfolio* records and reports stock purchases, commissions, divdends and splits. *Quotations* automatically updates the stocks in your portfolio each time you access the Dow Jones service. *PBL Corporation*

Securities Analysis—This program offers a wide variety of securities analysis techniques. Important tools such as stock analysis, call options, option spreads, bond analysis, calculations of compound interest, annuities and variable cash flow are included.

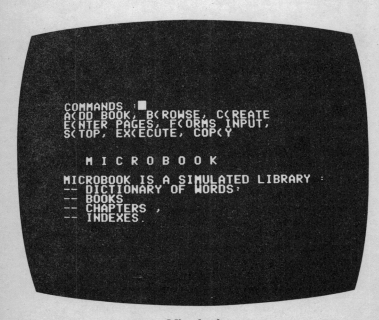

Microbook

Microbook: Database Management for the Apple II Computer—A database management program allows you to store, retrieve, and process data stored in files. This means that you can mix a large group of files that have different applications. This DBMS can be used for almost any application involving storage and retrieval of information—real estate records, accounting, stock market histories, mailing lists, or anything else you want to access. *dilithium Software*

Physicians Office Computer—This is a field tested software package for medical billing and patient data. The software automatically produces all of your statements, insurance forms, ledgers, recall notices, etc. *Professional Systems Corp.*

DAS (Dental Accounting System)—*DAS* and its counterparts *OAS* (Orthodontic Accounting System) and *VAS* (Veterinary Accounting System) proceduralize daily operations. It allows you to process all charges and payments through *ticket*

```
S TO SCREEN PRINT
L(OR J) TO LINE  PRINT(JUSTIFY)
E TO EDIT
T TO TAB SET              2 FOR FILE SIZE
G FOR CONDENSED  LINE PRINT
H FOR DBL SPACED CONDENSED  LINE PRINT
I FOR TPL SPACED CONDENSED  LINE PRINT
P FOR END OF PAGE
D TO ENTER NEW DISK MATERIAL
A TO  APPEND NEW DISK MATERIAL
Q FOR DISK   OUTPUT
K TO APPEND FROM KEYBOARD
M FOR MULTIPLE DISK PRINTING
V FOR MULTIPLE JUSTIFIED DISK PRINTING
Z TO RETURN TO DOS
```

Executive Assistant

entry programs by patient. Diagnostic and procedure codes are maintained as well as industry specific information. *Cimmarron*

Executive Assistant—Are you unsure about word processing? Do you know what it can do and how you can use it? This package could answer those questions for you. The package includes the program on disk, a user's manual, and a book, *The Tenderfoot's Guide to Word Processing.* The program contains all of the standard editing features; e.g., global search and replace, compact file storage, automatic pagination, etc. *dilithium Software*

Savvy—This is the program to end programming. You can use plain English commands to define parameters, then *Savvy* writes a program based on your parameters. *Excalibur Technologies*

Savvy

CHAPTER 3

How to Buy
Your Own Computer

Not long ago a student in one of our courses on small computers announced that she and her husband had taken the plunge. They had ordered their own computer! Thinking everyone we knew was in the same state of inflationary poverty that has a long term lease on our bank accounts, we assumed the happy owners had scraped together enough to get one of the $299 specials. Actually, the cost of their system was well over $2000. They had purchased one of the popular systems with dual disk drives, extra memory, a printer, and several hundred dollars worth of programs.

Why would a middle-class family spend $2000 on a computer system? This family had several reasons. They enjoyed games and felt the variety available for the computer they purchased would keep them entertained for years. The computer would also serve as a home tutor for the children. As a high school teacher, the wife wanted the computer to keep track of her pupils' records. Both she and her husband were looking forward to learning BASIC, and both had several ideas they hoped to turn into working programs.

Is this the typical "computer family"? Not really. In fact, there is no such thing as typical in this field. Most potential buyers want to use their computer for one or two major applications. Those *major* applications are the ones used to justify buying the computer in the first place. A friend of ours, for example, is a research psychologist at a center for retarded adults. He writes a number of articles and monographs each year. He bought his computer to analyze data and to serve as a word processing system.

For most people, there will be some, perhaps many, secondary reasons for buying a computer. These secondary reasons aren't enough by themselves to justify buying a computer. Many times, though, the secondary uses actually take up more of a computer's time than the major ones. The research psychologist and his family, for example, use their computer for recreational as well as professional applications.

STEPS IN SELECTING A SYSTEM

The process of buying a computer is complicated a bit by the number of options available. Buying a microwave oven or a color television is much simpler since they are single function devices. Computers, on the other hand, can do many things:

Computers find many uses in the home

they can entertain, teach, keep financial records, and much, much more. Not all the computers available, however, do everything equally well. Therefore, the first major step in selecting a computer is to identify the jobs you want done.

Step One. Identify Major Uses—It may seem simplistic and obvious to say you need to decide just what you want the computer to do. You would probably be surprised, though, at the number of people who buy a computer with only a vague idea of exactly how they will use it. Suppose you visit a local computer store and take a fancy to a particular computer. It shows well in the store, the programs are well written, they execute with little if any difficulty, and the results are in excellent color with quality graphics. After you buy the system you may decide that your primary use will be word processing with games as a secondary use. Unfortunately, you may find that the computer you bought is very good for games and educational uses, but virtually impossible to use as a word processor. In all likelihood, for the same amount of money you could have purchased a system that is very good for word processing and acceptable or even good for games and recreational uses.

The first step, then, is the most important. Decide what your major uses will be. Once that's clear, it will be easier to identify the computer systems that are capable of doing the work you want done. Several of the chapters in this book discuss many potential uses of a computer.

Step Two. Software Considerations—A computer will not do anything until it has a program (a set of instructions) to follow. Computer programs or *software* can be obtained in two ways. You can write your own programs or you can buy *canned* programs that are written by someone else. Many people do a little of both. They may buy most of the programs they regularly use, and write their own programs for specialized applications.

If you plan to write your own programs, it will be important to look carefully at the languages the computer you are considering uses. Most personal computers can be programmed in BASIC, a very popular language today. In addition, other languages, such as PILOT, are available for some but not all personal computers. Chapter 8 covers computer languages and software in more detail.

If you don't yet know how to program a computer and want to learn, pay careful attention to the teaching aids available with each computer. Are the manuals clear and easy to understand? Can you get teaching aids such as computer assisted instruction programs that help you learn the computer language you will use? Do you have a choice of languages and are there published books that support the computer?

Although learning to program a computer can be both interesting and very useful, a large percentage of the people who use personal computers today cannot write their own programs. Instead, they buy programs written by others. Many of us, for example, can't play a note, but that doesn't keep us from buying and enjoying records, albums, and tapes.

If you plan to buy programs for the computer you select, be sure there are programs to buy. There are a few computers which have gained such wide acceptance that many different companies sell all sorts of programs for them. Since, without software, a computer is just a bunch of parts, the variety and quality of software available for a particular computer becomes an important point to consider *before* you buy a system.

With most of the major small computers, you will probably be able to buy at least one or two programs in each of the major applications areas. Newer computers, and those from less well accepted manufacturers, however, may not have attracted as much interest from independent programmers, and there is no guarantee that a large number of suitable programs will be available.

Unfortunately, the newer machines tend to be the ones with the most sophisticated features. You may thus be caught in a dilemma that pits an older model with lots of software against a new model with many desirable features. Fortunately, the manufactuers are beginning to recognize this problem. Most invest a substantial amount of money and corporate energy in developing a large software selection for their computers. They may, for example, hire a large number of in-house programmers. Or they may make it very easy for independent programmers to get help in writing programs for their new models. In addition, many new systems are software compatible with older, more established models. Several new Commodore computers, for instance, can use programs developed for earlier models. The Franklin Ace 100, on the other hand, will run all the software developed for the Apple II. If you are shopping for a computer for your business, the term *CP/M compatible* may be music to your ears since there are thousands of business programs that will run on computers that are CP/M compatible.

Regardless of the method, any computer you buy should have a range of software available for the applications areas of interest to you.

Step Three. Specify Minimum Requirements and Preferred Features—Once you clearly specify the major uses, you will need to identify the features a computer must have to do those jobs. Some computers have a small *calculator*-style keyboard rather than a *typewriter*-style keyboard. It is very difficult on such keyboards to touch type, a necessity if you plan to use the computer for word processing. An appropriate keyboard is just the first of a number of minimum requirements for word processing. There must, of course, be a good word processing program available for the computer. It would be nice to have a video display that can put 24 lines of 80 characters on the screen at one time. Computers with that capacity are generally priced in the $2000 plus range, however. You can do very nicely with a display of 24 lines of 40 characters or 16 lines of 62 characters (but not with 22 lines of 23 characters). Several computers with the 24 by 40 or 16 by 62 format are available for around $1000.

None of the requirements noted above for word processing is essential, perhaps not even desirable, in a computer that is to be used solely for entertainment. Instead, you may want to consider characteristics such as whether the computer has a color video display, high quality graphics, many recreational programs, and provisions for plugging in game controllers. The final section of this chapter discusses a number of potential characteristics or features for computers. Few people will find all of them equally important. Your intended uses will determine which features are crucial, which are important, and which are of little importance.

Step 4. Identify Likely Secondary Uses and Desirable Machine Features—Suppose you've narrowed your choice of computers down to two systems. Both will do your major jobs well, both cost around $1100 with accessories. The choice may come down to the secondary use capabilities. For example, if your family has a strong interest in music, you may want to consider the music generation programs available for the two computers. If one computer has built-in features that allow you to compose and play music and several excellent music software packages, it may get the nod over the other one. Even if you don't buy the programs that let you express your musical talents when you buy the computer, it might be a good idea to buy the computer that allows you to add this feature later.

Step 5. Decide How Much You Want to Spend—Now and Later—Now comes the crunch. Unless you have large amounts of "disposable" income, you will have to compromise when you reach Step 5. It is possible today to buy a complete, fully functional computer for $79 to over $2 million. Personal computers generally cost between $300 and $3000 with most of the popular systems selling for between $200 and $1500.

(An exception is the Sinclair ZX81 which sells briskly for under $50. See Chapter 10 for more details.)

In the last three years, we've been involved in buying over 200 different computer systems either personally, through our business or university, or as consultants. In virtually every case, had we been able to spend $500 to $1000 more, we would have selected a different computer. The $1000 PET and the $3000 NorthStar computers, for example, can both be used to do similar jobs. The NorthStar, however, does many of them better, and has features (e.g., disk storage) that are optional extras on the PET. With some exceptions, you get useful features for the money you pay when it comes to buying a computer. The trick is to spend the money on the features you need. Don't spend money for something you don't need, and don't waste money buying a computer that doesn't have the features required for your application.

Another price consideration is how much you may have to spend later. We know of an owner who purchased a system for a very good price only to discover that the cost of expanding that system was very high. If, at some time in the future, you plan to buy additional equipment for your computer, be sure the cost will be reasonable.

Finally, a potential shock for the new owner is the cost of service. Some companies maintain regional repair centers that provide good service at a fair price. Others train and support dealers who provide service locally. A few manufacturers have little or no service. The owner of one such orphan system was told that even minor service would cost $120 plus parts each time a service person looked at the equipment. This may be typical and expected in the business world where large, complicated systems must be kept at peak operating efficiency, but small computer owners are likely to find the cost excessive.

Step 6. Try Them Out—Now that you know how you want to use a computer and have a fairly good idea of what is affordable, you can begin the tire-kicking phase. Chapter 11 contains descriptions of most of the major small computers that will be available at the beginning of 1983. It is only a starting place, however, since new and improved models are being introduced on a fairly regular basis. More up-to-date information can be obtained by visiting local computer stores (and other stores that handle personal computers) and from reading current issues of magazines such as *Interface Age*, *Microcomputing*, *Creative Computing*, *Compute*, *Infoworld*, *Personal Computing*, and *Popular Computing*.

We suggest you limit yourself to computers already on the market rather than those announced as being available *in the near future*. In this industry the near future can be as far away as three years. In some cases, new models are announced (and orders are accepted) for computers that are never produced. For instance, Mattel, the toy manufacturer, began selling a heavily advertised video game a few years ago. Mattel's advertisements and press releases indicated there would soon be an additional keyboard component that would turn the game into a full-fledged computer. Mattel's availability dates turned out to be overly optimistic, and when the keyboard unit did finally appear it was priced much higher than some complete computers.

The same sort of problem can occur with computer accessories. If you want a computer with a compatible printer from the same company, for example, look only at systems with acceptable printers already available and working rather than systems for which a fantastic printer is "in the works." One final point, no amount of reading reviews will take the place of a hands-on demonstration.

Step 7. Survey Sources—Steps 6 and 7 probably should be completed at the same time. As you check out computers for suitability, also evaluate the potential sources of supply. Most computers are purchased from one of three sources: a local retail store, a mail order supplier, or the manufacturer. Fewer and fewer manufacturers are willing to sell directly to consumers. Most prefer instead to deal with distributors and dealers who, in turn, sell to consumers. This frees the factory to concentrate on production and development. They then count on their dealers or separate service centers to provide most of the customer service.

Mail order is a mixed bag. There are excellent examples of ethical, responsible mail order businesses but there are also examples of plain crooks, inept ne'er-do-wells, and fast buck Olympians. If you are considering buying a computer that is supposed to be serviced by the retailer, a good local store with a top-notch technician who provides timely service is a valuable commodity. Prices at such a store may be a bit higher than they are from mail order discounters, but many people feel the extra price is worth it to have the person responsible for the warranty just down the street.

If you're not sure about a store, take the time to get opinions from computer owners in your area. We once considered buying an Apple II from a local dealer so we could get quick service. You can imagine how we felt when we discovered the dealer had no service personnel at all for Apple computers. When an Apple went down (needed repair) it was shipped back to the factory in California. Since the dealer's price for an Apple was $200 more than the mail order price, we reconsidered the purchase. Apparently many other people did the same. The store is no longer in business.

Even if you plan to buy a computer that has its own service centers, a local store can be a source of information and a place to try out different models before buying. Millions, however, live in towns or rural areas where there is no computer store, or the local store is so poor it does not justify the extra cost of buying locally.

Few generalizations can be made about mail order computer

companies. Some have good track records and some don't. Many mail order suppliers have a staff of service technicians and provide timely repair service. Others are slow at delivering goods in the first place and even slower at handling service requests. One way to protect yourself is to read the letters and commentaries about mail order companies in the computer magazines and talk with other computer owners in your area who purchase equipment by mail. In general, the less you know about computers the stronger our recommendation would be to buy locally *if* local service and support are included in the price.

Step 8. Buy It—There's not much else to say. Once you've done your homework go out and buy yourself a computer!

POTENTIALLY IMPORTANT FEATURES

Video Displays

All the popular home computer models use a video display for normal operation of the computer. All video displays are not created equal, however. Some computers display as few as 12 lines of text on the screen at one time and have 32 or fewer characters on each line. That is a little on the skimpy side. The standard displays for small computers can put either 24 lines of 40 characters or 16 lines of 64 characters on the screen at once. Premium and business systems generally use a 24 by 80 format.

For recreational computing, educational applications, and some business applications two other features, color and graphics, are more important than the character display capacity. Several models now offer color displays rather than the traditional black and white. Color adds zest to games and makes computer-aided learning more interesting.

Most computers also have at least some graphics capability. That means, in addition to letters and numbers, the computer can display figures, graphs, charts, game boards, or computer generated pictures on the screen. On some computers such as the TRS-80 Model IV the graphics features are limited but useful. The ATARI computers and the IBM PC, on the other hand, can handle very sophisticated graphics. In addition to educational and game applications, businesses can use color graphics to create sales displays as well as charts and figures.

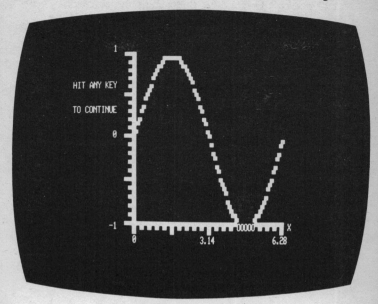

An example of computer graphics

Three other points should be made about video displays. First, while most computers have video display capacity, many do not come with video monitors. Some are designed to be connected to a standard television, and some require you to buy a video monitor. Monitors cost from $125 to $900 depending on their quality and whether the monitor is color or black and white. Second, while all systems will display letters and numbers, some display only upper-case (capital) letters. The TRS-80 Color Computer, for example, is an upper-case only machine. We prefer a display with both upper- and lower-case letters, but your pattern of usage will determine how important that feature is.

The final point to remember about displays has to do with the quality of the color graphics. You may read advertisements which state such and such a computer has a display of "280 by 192 pixels." Essentially, that means the screen has been divided into 280 rows and 192 columns. Each point where a row and column intersect is called a *pixel*, and the computer is capable of controlling what is displayed at that location. The larger the number of pixels in a display the finer or more precise the display can be. A circle drawn on a computer with 80 by 50 graphics will look ragged while a computer with 360 by 192 graphics will display a much smoother, more pleasing circle. Several computers allow you to choose the quality of the graphics you use, from rather coarse graphics to fine-grained video pictures. In addition, computers vary in terms of the number of colors which can be simultaneously displayed on the screen.

Sound

Several popular computers have no built-in sound generation at all. Others can generate crude buzzes and a narrow range of useful sounds, and a few have built-in sound synthesizers that create a variety of sophisticated sounds (including music) in several voices. Depending on your application, sound may be unimportant or crucial. If it is important, look for a system that

Produces sound in several voices.
Is capable of generating many different notes.
Can create different tonal qualities.
Has an adjustable volume level.
Uses easy to understand commands.

Sound generation should be a function of BASIC or some other easy to use language.

If your primary interest is computer generated music, the built-in sound features on most small computers will not be sophisticated enough for serious applications. In that case, you may want to look at the add-on equipment currently available for the different computers. The Apple II, for example, is a popular computer for music buffs because several companies manufacture synthesizers and keyboards for it.

Keyboard

Perhaps we're fanatics about keyboards, but they can determine whether working with the computer is a joy or a pain. Three manufacturers, Commodore (PET), Sinclair, and Texas Instruments, saw fit to produce computers with midget-sized keyboards resembling those on calculators. The keys are small and closely spaced. They are not our cup of tea. If you have big fat fingers like we do, they are hard to use without making errors, and there is no way to touch type on these tiny keyboards. Commodore now offers a full-size keyboard on even its least expensive machine and TI has retired its undersized keyboard for a larger (but still undersized) one. Sinclair, on the other hand, has priced their computer so low that many are willing to put up with the inconvenience of the small hunt-and-peck keyboard.

The sight of a full-sized typewriter-style keyboard on your intended computer does not mean all is well, however. A good keyboard should offer smooth resistance to the touch without catching, and the whole assembly should be firmly mounted with no flexing. Finally, the keyboard should be free of *key-bounce*. You have keybounce when you type an A on the

ASCII keyboard

keyboard and AA or AAA appears on the screen. Keyboards with contact points exposed to dust are particularly susceptible to keybounce. The early Model I TRS-80s win the prize for the most keybounce. After a West Texas dust storm, some of our TRS-80s were virtually unusable. Tandy wisely scrapped its original keyboard in the middle of 1980 and now uses a very good one on its Model 12 and Model IV computers.

The ATARI 400 uses a standard size, touch-sensitive membrane keyboard. The keyboard on the 400 is functional but inexpensive, and the much lower price of the 400 is possible partially because of the membrane keyboard. The membrane keyboards are fine for games and for running canned programs. They are not so fine for word processing (don't even try) or for projects that require you to spend many hours writing programs or entering data. Before selecting a computer, we suggest you sit down at the keyboard and work with it for a while. Consider your probable uses for the system and decide whether the keyboard will be acceptable to you.

Power Supply

Most of the power supplies in current models are at least adequate. The virtues and vices of power supplies are discussed in more detail in Chapter 9. There is one problem, however, that should be discussed here. Several of the popular systems

today use the *component* model. That is, the computer itself
is a separate unit which can be purchased by itself. You may
then pick and choose from a wide range of accessories to
complete your system. Several of these component systems
have a separate power supply for each component. It is not
very difficult to end up with as many as six or seven different
power supplies, each of which must be plugged into a wall
socket or extension cord and also plugged into a computer
component. It is very difficult to make these systems look neat,
and all those cords dangling everywhere invite an accident.
The advantage of the component approach, however, is that
you can install new accessories yourself. Texas Instruments
recently changed from a component approach to a modular
system. They now sell a component *chassis* for their TI 99/
4A computer. Most accessories are inserted into slots in the
component chassis which has its own power supply and one
power cord. That approach may be preferable although the
expense of the chassis means you will spend more to add your
first accessories than someone using a component system.

Storage Medium Options

Virtually all personal computers come with cassette storage
systems. Programs or data you want to save and use later can
be recorded on regular (but good quality) audio cassettes. Cassette storage is cheap, often reliable, and easy to use. Unfortunately, it is slow. A large program can take as long as five
minutes or more to load. That may not sound like a long time
now, but when you're sitting in front of the computer it can
be forever, particularly if there are problems with the load and
you have to do it again...and again...and again. It is also
easy to end up with a hundred or more tapes scattered around
the computer. Finding the one you need can take longer than
a visit to the dentist (and be nearly as painful). Actually, we
should not be so negative about cassette storage. Good systems
can be very pleasant and easy to use. A poorly designed one,
however, is very trying.

Fortunately most computer systems today have at least pass-
able cassette systems. The worst offenders, when it comes to
reliable cassette systems, are gone now. Even those with rep-

utations for poor operation (e.g., the TRS-80 Model I) have had their circuit designs modified and improved considerably. The TRS-80 Model III, the ATARI 800 and 400, the Commodore PETs, and many other models all seem to work dependably.

A popular alternative to cassette storage is the *floppy disk*. Floppy disks are fast, very reliable, and as you might expect, expensive. Count on paying at least $500, perhaps as much as $900, for a small single drive system. Dual drive systems cost even more. For the money, you get a high speed, reliable storage system that can put many programs on each of the little 5¼-inch disks. Many computers for businesses have built-in disk drives in lieu of cassette systems. They are generally in the $3000+ price range, but they give businesses the speed and storage capacity required for large scale applications. Disks can also be added to most of the personal computers as well. If you can afford them, they are the preferred storage system for small computers today.

5¼-inch disk drive

Actually disks come in two sizes (5¼-inch and 8-inch). The capacity of the disks vary according to size and type, but a great deal of data can be stored on even the smallest, least sophisticated disk drive. While there have been some quality control problems with a few of the drive manufacturers, the level of quality in floppy disk systems is reasonably high.

Another increasingly popular storage system is the hard disk. These devices are even more expensive than floppy disks, but offer increased speed and a huge storage capacity. The smallest hard disk drives available today are capable of storing 5 million characters. Prices, however, begin at around $3000.

Base Cost and Expansion Costs

It is probably natural to compare computer prices by looking at the price tag on the keyboard, but that may not tell all the story. Consider a familiar example. When you shop for a new car, the sticker prices on two cars can vary by as much as $5000 even when both cars are on the same dealer lot and are the same make and model. The difference in sticker price can be accounted for by options. One may have air conditioning, power steering and brakes, a moon roof, special accent and protective molding, a special engine and transmission, special paint job, and an optional AM/FM stereo cassette player. The same thing can happen with computers. One dealer may quote you a very low price for a computer while another dealer may offer to sell you a system for hundreds of dollars more. The higher bid may mean the dealer has listened to you describe what you want to do with your computer and is offering a system that includes all the accessories needed to do that job.

There is the *base* price of the computer and there is the cost of *expanding* the computer to do a particular job. The base price may not include the cost of a cassette recorder, disk drive, extra memory, or a printer. Many first time buyers of computers are shocked to find that the cost of accessories can easily add up to several times the cost of the computer itself. We are used to buying a $7000 car and looking at options and accessories that cost only a fraction of the cost of the car. With a computer it is possible to buy disk drive systems or printers that cost much more than the computer. That means the base price of the computer is not very important to many people. The important number is the cost of expanding the system to do the work you want it to do. It would be easy for a company to put a very competitive price on their computer to attract buyers and then to make the cost of expanding the system very high. This has been done by several companies.

The point is, always consider the cost of expanding a basic system to meet your specific needs, not just the price of a bare bones computer. A related point has to do with the source of your expansion accessories. The Radio Shack Model III computer, for example, can be purchased for around $900 without a disk drive system. Radio Shack currently retails their disk drive add-on kit for around $900 plus installation. On the other hand, several other suppliers offer disk drive add-ons for as little as $500. You can save quite a bit by not buying accessories for many computers from the manufacturer. If you do that, however, you may void the warranty on your computer (if it hasn't already expired) and the authorized service center may be unwilling to work on the system if it needs repair (because it has foreign accessories). Finally, while companies such as VR Data and PERCOM have established reputations for reliable products that some of the manufacturers should envy, there are some companies selling poorly designed, poorly supported products that are better left on the shelf. You will have to decide if the money saved is worth the risk and potential problems.

User Friendliness

Although the term "user friendly" has become a cliche today, it does refer to a very important concept. Some computers are designed with the user in mind. They are friendly, easy to use, run reliably, and require very little effort to begin using them. The ease of use factor can be an important one. Look at the way the computer is designed, the placement of keys on the keyboard, the location of important switches, and look at the documentation that comes with the computer. Is it easy to read? Does it cover everything you need to know to use the computer? A user friendly computer is worth a lot more than a computer that has the same capabilities but is difficult to use.

Accessories Available

If you browse through current issues of several popular computer magazines you will find hundreds of ads for all sorts of products which make life in front of your computer easier, more convenient, more efficient, more enjoyable, or more profitable. Some computers are popular enough to attract the attention of many different companies who manufacture computer peripherals. There may be speech recognition and speech synthesis systems, music synthesizers, high quality graphics generators, modified game paddles, extra memory boards, several different disk drive systems, and on and on. If the manufacturer offers many different accessories and there are other suppliers of equipment for the computer as well, you will not only have many options to choose from, the competition is likely to keep prices lower than they would be if there were fewer suppliers.

After Sale Support

Is there a toll-free number you can call for information and help with your computer? Is there a local and/or national users group? Does the company support a magazine about the computer? Is the computer popular enough to support independent magazines devoted to articles about the computer? The more questions you can answer "yes" to the more after sale support you have.

CHAPTER 4

The Home Computer

We are frequently asked the question "What can I do with a computer?" It is a simple question, but one that is very difficult to answer for a particular person or family. The computer is much like an artist's blank canvas or a sculptor's block of stone. The outcome will depend on the artist or the user. In this chapter we will try to give you an idea of what other people are doing with computers. What you do is up to you.

ENTERTAINMENT

Many people say they are buying their computer for other reasons, but the A-number-one use of computers in the home is fun. That is not to say the computers aren't used for other things like checkbook balancing. They are. But you only balance your checkbook when you have to. It's not something you look forward to after a long day at the office. Playing games, composing music, or drawing color pictures on the screen are lots more fun. The checks can wait until tomorrow night.

Within the category of entertainment, there are several different types of computer activities. Action-oriented games that use color graphics and sound to the fullest are very popular today. Most are based on a similar premise. You are in charge of a space ship, laser cannons on earth, or something else that will allow you to protect yourself and civilization from some dreaded threat to freedom. To do your job, you must blow up as many of them as possible. However, they can blow you up too, so be careful. Many of these games make use of *joysticks* or *game paddles* instead of the computer's keyboard. It is generally easier to shoot down invading alien starships with a joystick than by typing commands on the keyboard. The action-oriented games are fast-paced, require quick reaction times, and are totally engrossing for a large segment of the population.

Several computers can run games strikingly similar to the arcade games that cost a quarter to play. There are virtually thousands of action games to play on personal computers today. The violence in some of these games has been criticized by some on the grounds that it leads to greater violence in real life. That may or may not be true. Over twenty years of research of the impact of television violence on children's behavior is thus far relatively inconclusive. There are some indications, however, that children who are already prone to aggressive behavior are influenced by violence on television (in a negative way) while children without such tendencies are not. Other studies suggest that watching programs that encourage and reward polite behavior lead to more polite behavior on the part of some students. There is very little research on the effect of playing *Space Invaders* (Atari) ten thousand times, however.

Another type of game that is popular today is the *strategy* game. A typical example is a game called *Deadline* (Infocom). You are a detective who must investigate a murder and solve it in 12 hours. You are given a complete set of clues and you may conduct your investigation in any way you please. There are, of course, some devious, shady characters who may do you in if you make a wrong move. Strategy games focus on thinking skills and on the ability to logically solve the problems posed.

IBM Personal Computer

Eastern Front (Atari) is another strategy game that puts you in command of an army during World War II. Eastern Front runs on the Atari computers. The game displays a map (actually several maps) of Western Russia and identifies the locations of your troops. You must make all sorts of decisions about deployment of troops, allocation of resources, and decisions about when, where and how to attack or retreat. The program takes into consideration the type of terrain, the season (winters are just as bad as they were for Napoleon), and the quality of the forces arrayed against you. In addition, if you formulate your strategy quickly and act on it without delay, the enemy does not react as intelligently as they will if you take a long time to act.

Another popular type of recreational program is one that simulates a card game or Las Vegas specials such as roulette. Virtually every card game known to humans has been programmed on a computer. In one version of poker, for example, a shifty-eyed dealer gives you your hand and takes care of the house's money when you win or lose. There are even programs that tutor you in how to play popular card games so you won't lose so quickly the next time you go to Las Vegas or Atlantic City.

Simulations of competitive team sports like football, baseball, and basketball are also popular computer games. You can play a world series or a playoff series right on your computer keyboard. Some of the sports simulation programs are strategy games in that you must decide what plays to run. Others are action games where you use joysticks or game controllers to direct your team on the court or playing field.

Board games such as chess, checkers, and tic-tac-toe are also available for most popular small computers. Several versions of computer chess can actually beat many novice players with ease when the program is set to its most intelligent level. Atari has a 3D version of tic-tac-toe that is a challenging game that requires attention to play on several levels. You can play against someone else or the computer. Play against the computer is also possible with the *Computer Chess* program from Atari. The computer displays a chessboard in color and then plays against you at any of seven levels of difficulty. Chess pieces are moved by tilting the joystick in the direction you want a piece to move. At the higher levels of difficulty the computer can be hard to beat.

There are so many different recreational programs available for small computers today that this brief overview only hints at the possibilities. The program racks at your local computer store are likely to have many more on display, and the computer magazines regularly carry ads for hundreds more. One magazine, *Softside* (515 Abbott Drive, Bromall, Pa. 19008) publishes recreational programs every month for the TRS-80, Apple II, and ATARI computers. The magazine publishes other types of programs as well. If you don't like typing in programs, *Softside* also sells its programs on diskettes or cassettes. Many of the magazines described in the last chapter of this book also publish recreational programs you can type in and use.

PERSONAL DEVELOPMENT

The computer can be a very effective learning tool. We have devoted an entire chapter to educational computing. Chapter 6 describes many more educational applications; some of these are also appropriate for home use (e.g., a touch typing course and foreign language programs) while others are more likely to be used in schools.

Several computers have programs that teach you how to program a computer. Many families, in fact, learn about computer programming as a family since everyone is starting at ground zero. Programs are also available to teach you a variety of topics from pre-school shape discrimination to college-level physics.

PERSONAL FINANCE AND RECORD KEEPING

Well, we've finally come to the work. With a computer, however, it should be easier to balance your checkbook, keep track of investments, or put your coin collection in order. There are programs to help computer owners do virtually all of their financial record keeping. Below are short descriptions of a few illustrative applications:

Budgeting and Checkbook Balancing

A personal budgeting program helps a family keep track of spending and earning patterns. The more involved programs can even provide an overview of spending and earning trends. Monthly and yearly printouts on spending categories and predicted patterns can be generated. Each month when checks are written to pay bills, the computer can speed up the process by providing a display of recurring payments (e.g., mortgage, car payment) as well as incidental bills (e.g., car repairs, gasoline credit card bills and others that vary from month to month). The computer can keep track of bills received, payments made, and information such as the time between receipt and payment, the minimum payment due, the total owed on each account, and the interest paid on each account.

Less ambitious programs just help the family bill payer balance the checkbook when the monthly statement arrives from the bank. The typical checkbook balancing program uses a screen display to organize deposits and disbursements, and asks you to type in the amount of each check written or deposit made. It then checks your input against the bank statement and identifies any discrepancies. This can save an hour or two each month and helps spot any mistakes you or the bank made.

Investment and Tax Programs

A financial record keeping program leads naturally to the question of whether computers can do anything to uncomplicate that annual American ritual of offering financial sacrifices to the IRS god. Yes, it can. The computer, for example, can keep track of tax deductible payments and purchases made during a year and provide you with a categorized list with totals at tax time. This one application has saved some owners the cost of the computer. Several software companies also sell income tax software that actually compute your tax each year and fill out the 1040 forms.

```
                  C H E C K   E N T R Y

  ACCT #...1           NAME..FT. WORTH BANK & TRUST

  CK. ID...000011    DATE..10/17/81   AMOUNT...   20.00

                      TYPE..M  (P=PRINT, M=MANUAL)
  TO THE
  ORDER OF..16  John M. Williams
                5623 S.W. Greenville
                Ft. Worth            TX 76123


  FOR.......00  Services Rendered    LAST PAYEE...

   ENTER SELECTION..I  (A=ADD, C=CHANGE, D=DELETE, I=INQUIRY)
  DISPLAY NEXT CHECK? Y/N   ■
```

A check entry program

The computer can also be used to help you make good investment decisions. Several software publishers market programs that can be used to manage a portfolio of stocks. Most will calculate the rate of return for each stock on an annual and long term basis, and evaluate a stock in terms of the projected dividend payments it is likely to yield in the future. Other programs keep track of a stock's performance across days, months, and years and generate commonly used values that indicate how a stock is performing (i.e., price variations, number of shares being traded, high and low prices). The programs don't tell you whether to sell or keep a stock, but they do provide you with several important pieces of information which help you make decisions. Similar programs are available for bonds.

One program, *Stock Charting* (Atari), is used to keep track of a stock's performance across days, months, and years. It generates several commonly used values that indicate how a stock is performing (i.e., price variations, number of shares being traded, high and low prices). *Stock Charting* can be used to follow several stocks at once with performance data displayed in charts and tables.

If you're like us, you are more likely to be borrowing money than investing it these days. Another type of program provides detailed information on mortgages and loans. Such programs can be very useful if you are considering major purchases that must be financed. Recently, when Jerry bought a piece of real estate, his trusty mortgage interest rate books could not be used because they only went up to 12 percent, a figure that seemed almost criminal only a few years ago, and now would be much sought after if only it were available. Jerry used an inexpensive computer program to determine the monthly payments on mortgages at various interest rates (13¾ percent to 16½ percent) and on mortgages of varying lengths (20 to 30 years). The program will display information in charts on the screen or print a permanent copy if you have a printer. After considering the likely rate of inflation over the term of the loan, the tax relief provided by interest payments, and the options provided by accepting a favorable second mortgage from the seller, Jerry was able to make an offer that was both financially manageable and economically sound. Using the program considerably reduced the amount of tedious figuring required to compare the many alternatives.

We really have touched only on the more obvious financial applications in this section. There are programs that help you make a decision on whether to buy a particular piece of rental property, programs that manage and keep track of real estate investments, programs that keep track of family property and many, many more. There is likely to be an even wider variety of programs in the future. If financial applications are of particular interest to you, read Chapter 7 on business applications.

HOBBY AND RECREATIONAL PROGRAMS

In addition to the games already discussed under "entertainment," many people use a computer in their hobbies. An Oklahoma friend of ours, Jerry Scott, is a computer dealer and a motorcycle rider. Now he isn't one of those fellows who rides across the country on a big "hog" wearing a war surplus leather jacket. His group sponsors a type of competitive race called an *enduro*. It is aptly named because it involves trying to endure riding over 100 miles through swamps, over hills, into rivers, and under fences while maintaining a specified course speed. As in a car rally, riders start at different times and must arrive at specified check points along the way. A good enduro requires a large amount of record keeping which must be done with to-the-second precision. Our Oklahoma friend wrote an enduro scoring program for his computer that not only helps ensure accuracy, it actually scores the race and prints out the winners quicker than was ever possible before.

You may not be interested in using a computer to score motorcycle races, but it is very likely that a computer can be used in some aspect of your favorite hobby. Chapter 5 tells you how to use the computer to check airline schedules and make vacation or business reservations for flights, car rentals, and hotel rooms. If you have an extensive collection of stamps, coins, records, etc., you can use a computer to keep a categorized and catalogued inventory of your collection.

If you belong to a club, religious group, or any organization with many members, you can use a computer's word processing talents to write and print a newsletter. Then you can use a mailing list program to keep track of members' addresses and to print mailing labels for each issue. A mailing list program can be used to print mailing labels, keep a Christmas card list, keep track of the addresses and phone numbers of family and friends, and for many other purposes. It can even be used to organize information that has nothing to do with addresses. A family with a large collection of tools in many different locations (e.g., basement workshop, garage, summer cottage, office) can use the program to keep an inventory of tools along with their location. Most mailing lists programs have features that permit you to get a listing (on the screen or on a printer) of selected categories (e.g., all the tools at the summer cottage, all relatives living in Tennessee, club members with specific interests, etc.).

We could write an entire book on hobby applications of computers, but the examples above should give you an idea of the range of possibilities. Current issues of many computer magazines such as *Popular Computing*, *Creative Computing*, *Interface Age*, and *Personal Computing* will usually have articles about other uses in this category.

HOME CONTROL

We have included this category of application because it is frequently discussed in popular magazines and in newspaper articles about computing. A typical article will describe how a computer can be programmed to keep the house at a certain temperature, how it can turn on the coffee pot a few minutes before you get up in the morning, and so on. A computer can, indeed, be programmed to control the environment in your home. It will keep the temperature just right, water the begonias when their soil is dry, and circulate air through the solar collectors when the sun is shining and the house is cold. The problem with this scenario, however, is one of overkill. The coffee pot can be turned on by a $4.95 timer just as well as by a $500 computer. In fact, all the computer applications which fall under the general category of "home control" will probably be performed, not by a general purpose computer, but by a *dedicated* computer.

Many microwave ovens, for example, have computers in them that control operation of the oven. That computer is dedicated to one job, controlling the oven, and probably costs the oven manufacturer $5 to $15. Some "smart" thermostats also have dedicated computers in them. Dedicated computers are less expensive, and their operation does not tie up a general purpose computer. Using a $500 personal computer as an intelligent burglar alarm is certainly possible, but the computer could not be used for anything else while it is watching for burglars. We, therefore, do not expect to see general purpose computers widely used in home control applications in spite of newspaper articles and the appearance of a few model "homes of the future" that use them for that purpose.

COMPUTERS AND HEALTH

This last category of home applications has been given very little attention thus far, but it is one we believe will increase in the future. The health problems of many individuals require them to follow precisely defined regimens of diet, exercise, or medicine. A computer, for example, has been used to keep track of a diabetic child's blood and urine glucose levels. The computer can also plot trends that indicate whether current insulin dosage levels are appropriate and warn the parents if a pattern indicates a problem. Exercise programs, diets, and other types of health-related projects can all be improved by using a computer to keep track of progress.

SUMMARY

This concludes our brief summary of home applications. As you can see, a computer can be put to work in a variety of ways in the home. It can also bring hours of enjoyment to family members of all ages. For additional ideas about how computers can be used in the home we suggest you read Chapter 6 on educational computing and Chapter 5 on the computer as a communications device.

CHAPTER 5

The Outer Limits: Communicating with the World

A computer can change the way you do things but can it also change the way you think about things? If you think of it as a communications device, it may very well do just that. Using the computer as a communications device is probably the least understood application today, yet it may be the use that introduces the largest number of people to computers. It may, in fact, have an impact on our way of life that parallels the impact of the television or the telephone.

Societies have always been concerned with information and with communication. Not only do we want to know, we want to know quickly. The original long distance Olympic runners, for example, were honored for their speed partially because they could carry messages quickly. The Pony Express, clipper ships, transatlantic cables, communications satellites, and the telegraph are familiar examples of advances that helped us to communicate better and faster.

We are now entering a new era of communication that may change not only the way we get and use information, but also the ways in which we communicate with each other. That new era, in fact, has already arrived for many. Farmers in Ohio, Texas, and Nebraska use small computers in their homes to get current prices and market trends on commodities they plan to buy or sell. At the same time, farmers are checking their markets, a stockbroker on the California coast may be checking stock prices with a computer connected to the television in his den, and a precious metals trader in Denver may be using her computer to get the Zurich, London, and New York gold and silver prices. The farmer, the stock broker, and the commodity trader all use the computer for two reasons. First, they get the information they need quickly, and second, they save time because the computer does much of the required clerical work. A third benefit for many computer owners is convenience. In some sections of the country, computers in the home are used to check on airline reservations, pay bills, look at movie reviews, get detailed weather forecasts, and display information and ads from local or out-of-town newspapers. In the near future, you will be able to go shopping by sitting down at your computer and selecting the items you want to purchase. You may even be able to compare prices in nearby stores without spending time and money driving to each store.

First-time buyers of computers are often unaware of the many potential uses of a computer as a communications device. Many current owners, however, use their computer regularly as a communications system, and the future is likely to bring a tremendous increase as new services become available.

Terms such as *electronic mail*, *teleconferencing*, *networks*, and *information management* are tossed about regularly today. When you finish reading this chapter, you will know what those terms actually mean and you will know how to use your computer as a communications device.

There are actually two ways that computers communicate with other computers. Many current applications use ordinary telephone lines to provide the link between your computer and another system. Actually, *line* is probably a misnomer since today most long distance phone calls are transmitted via land based microwave systems or relayed by satellite. We will use the term *phone line* to denote any of the new technology. The principle is still the same and the monthly bill still comes from the phone company.

In addition to systems that use the ordinary telephone lines, a few systems use cable television wires as a means of interconnection. Most of the examples in this chapter will take advantage of Ma Bell's technology, but more and more cities are adding cable services that can be connected to a personal computer.

MAJOR COMMUNICATIONS USES

Five major uses come to mind when we think of the computer as a communications device: information management, electronic mail, consumer services, programs, and computing.

Information Management

The computer can allow us to tap into all sorts of *electronic information banks* where data we want is sorted and stored. A doctor can check for information on a new disease; a stock broker can check the markets and a consumer can locate a store that sells a particular item or brand.

One of the earliest of the information utilities was the Prestel system developed and marketed in London by the British Post Office. There are some efforts to bring the British system to the U.S. as a commercial product, but Prestel is probably too expensive to become popular in the U.S. The special equipment required costs over $1000 and is not as versatile as a small computer that costs less.

Electronic Mail and Electronic Publishing

Members of most *networks* can write messages to other members. Each time you connect to the service it will indicate whether there are messages for you. In addition, there are numerous electronic bulletin boards or newsletters which contain special types of information. Network members, for example, who own a particular computer may be able to read notes and articles about their computer.

Consumer Services

Shopping by computer and paying bills by computer are two examples of consumer applications. The range of consumer services available in most areas is rather limited at present, but future users are likely to have their choice of many competing systems.

Experimental projects currently underway will allow you to sit at home and pay your bills by computer. One popular system to be discussed later in this chapter (The Source) plans a service called The Music Source that lets you select any of over 5000 records or tapes which are then charged to your credit card and delivered by UPS.

Another system jointly developed by Atari, Inc., Compu-Serve, and a cable television company called Qube seems almost like science fiction. The Qube network in Columbus, Ohio, will let you access stock markets, read movie reviews, do shopping and a lot of other things. All of the instructions for using the service are provided by the cable network. This revolutionary service, or something like it, will probably be available to you in a very few years.

Downloading Programs

Some services provide a list of computer programs available to users. If you want to buy one of these programs, the service will transmit, *download*, the program to your computer and bill you for the cost of the program at the end of the month. Once it is in the memory of your computer it is possible to make a copy of the program on a cassette tape or disk. Although this feature has been discussed and talked about for several years there are really very few programs that can be down-loaded at present. While there may be more in the future, it is by no means certain that downloading will become popular for software distribution.

Computing

It may seem redundant to say a computer can be used for computing, but this is a little different. One advantage of small computers is that they can be used by themselves (e.g., as *stand-alone* systems), but there may be times when you need to use the computing power of a gigantic $5 million computer. Most of us can't afford to buy such a machine, but a small computer in our home or office will allow us to connect to a big mainframe computer and use its computing power for a nominal charge.

In the next section of this chapter we will discuss in more detail some specific services available today. The two national networks, which will be discussed first, offer many different types of services. Other, more specialized or limited, services will be discussed in the final sections of the chapter.

PERSONAL COMPUTER NETWORKS

Currently there are two established national, general-purpose networks: The Source and CompuServe. Both can be used by anyone with a small computer, a credit card (so they can bill you monthly), and a telephone. The only special equipment required is a device called a *modem*. It allows you to connect the computer to the telephone line so you can transmit and receive information over the phone. Calls to the two major networks are local calls in many major cities. (If you live in a smaller city or in a rural area there may be an additional charge for each minute of *connect time*.)

The Source

The Source is a service of Source Telecomputing Corporation, 1616 Anderson Road, McLean, Virginia 22102 (703–821–6660).

If you want to sign up with The Source you can do so through the mail or at many computer stores. Like cable television there is an initial hookup charge. The charge is $100. After that, The Source charges $7.75 per off-peak hour (6PM–12AM) weekdays, all day weekends and holidays, $5.75 per hour (12AM–7AM) weekdays and weekends, and $20.75 per hour during prime time (7AM–6PM weekdays). There is a minimum monthly charge of $10 whether you use the system or not. The phone call to The Source is a local call in over 300 cities. Few people will want every service offered by The Source, but it's nice to know they're there. Some of the most interesting services are described below:

Consumer Services—With The Source, you can check airline schedules worldwide and make hotel, car rental, and airline reservations. There is a classified ad bulletin-board where you can check for bargains from all across the country (or sell a bargain yourself). In addition, there is a discount buying service that lets you select brand name products from the service and pay for them with your credit card. There is even a real estate service that helps you buy or sell a house.

Computer Services—The Source allows you to write and run programs in a variety of languages including BASIC, COBOL, and FORTRAN, among others. The Source also makes available quite a few canned programs of their own. Many are free; some involve a small charge. The programs available include games, business software, and software for special applications such as statistical analysis of large amounts of data. You cannot buy these programs and run them without being connected to The Source. In essence you *rent* them by connecting to The Source by phone and typing in the name of the program you want to use.

Data Bases—A service likely to be used by many subscribers is access to some of the many data bases available via The Source. One of the more popular data bases is the United Press International (UPI) wire service. It is possible to tell The Source to put the UPI output on the screen and watch the news scroll by on the screen. However, that is a very inefficient way of finding the news you're interested in. From your computer you can tell the UPI data base exactly which stories you want to read. If you want to find out what the latest happenings in the current crisis country are, you can do so by typing in the name of the country. All of the recent stories filed with UPI about that country will be displayed. It is easy to get in-depth reports on any subject you are interested in. Best of all, you can have up-to-date information any time you want it. The UPI data base is only one of a large number of data bases available on The Source. It takes some effort to learn how to use them effectively, but the effort is always worth it.

Electronic Mail—If you want to send a message or letter to another Source subscriber you can type it in on your keyboard and store it in the memory of The Source's computers. The next time that subscriber signs on, The Source will signal there is a message waiting. It is even possible to call a toll-free number and dictate a letter over the phone. Your letter will be put in the electronic mail file. Special interest groups can also use the electronic mail feature by placing information in a sort of electronic bulletin board that can be read by subscribers with similar interests.

The Source has had its growing pains, and it is currently a pale shadow of what will probably be available in the future. That said, however, it is still an amazing service and one that would have been impossible only a few years ago.

CompuServe

The major competitor to The Source is CompuServe Information Service, originally known as MicroNET. There are many similarities between the two and some differences. CompuServe charges only $30 initially, and charges $5 per hour during nonprime time (6PM to 5:30AM weekdays, all day weekends and holidays). CompuServe is not available during normal working hours since the company that runs this service uses its computers to serve commercial customers during that time. The connect call is local in over 260 cities.

CompuServe offers services similar to those of The Source. CompuServe has a somewhat better reputation than The Source for reliability and for faster response times. Instead of UPI, CompuServe uses the Associated Press newswire (as well as the *New York Times* service). CompuServe also offers information on topics as diverse as home repair, personal health, and recipes. Like The Source, it has book and movie reviews available as well as a sports information service. There is even a file of computer art that can be copied on your printer if you have one.

Like The Source, CompuServe has a number of financial data bases that you can use to investigate and track the stock and commodities markets. Choosing between The Source and CompuServe is difficult. The CompuServe package can be conveniently purchased at many Radio Shack stores or from

CompuServe (5000 Arlington Centre Boulevard, Columbus, Ohio 43220, 614–457–8600). Both services add new services regularly and both are reasonably priced. Therefore, you might want to sign up for both.

```
CompuServe                    Page 2

CompuServe Information Service

1 News, Weather, Sports
2 Finance
3 Entertainment
4 Electronic Mail
5 CompuServe User Information
6 Special Services
7 Home Information

9 MicroNET

Last menu page. Key digit
or M for previous menu.
```

CompuServe menu

Other Data Bases

In addition to the general purpose information supermarkets, there are many specialized services which offer a more limited range of services. What they lack in breadth, however, is more than offset by the depth of some of these services. Some financial services, for example, won't have any information on the weekend football games, but they can provide detailed information on the performance of thousands of corporations. Current stock prices and stock performance patterns are only a starting point. There is deep background information that covers the corporate history as well as recent news items relating to the corporation's products, management policies, merger possibilities, and technological status.

There are too many data bases to list all of them here. Many are very specialized and very expensive (as much as $85,000 per year plus connect time charges!). One source of additional information is the *Directory of On-Line Data Bases* ($60 a year for four issues) which is available in some libraries or from Cuadra Associates, Inc., 1523 Sixth Street, Suite 12, Santa Monica, California 90401. Another source of information that may be easier (and cheaper) to get, is an article in the April, 1981, issue of *Creative Computing* entitled "A Guide to Data Banks." In this section we will discuss one of the largest and most widely used data banks now in service.

Dialog—Graduate students and professors in many academic disciplines have used Dialog, a subsidiary of Lockheed Missile and Space Company (Lockheed Information Systems, 3251 Hanover Street, Palo Alto, California 94304, [415] 493-4411). Most major universities offer Dialog services through their libraries, but individuals can also subscribe to the service and be billed monthly. If you only use Dialog occasionally, you may find it easier to go to the library and get a specially trained librarian to talk to Dialog on your behalf. Dialog uses a rather complicated but powerful system of instructions to find exactly the information you need.

Dialog is not really one data base; it is over 75. There are data bases for chemists, patent attorneys, philosophers, special education teachers, anthropologists, physicians, and many, many others. When you talk to Dialog, one of the first things it wants to know is which data base you need to use. Once that is determined, you can tell Dialog exactly what you desire. As you work with Dialog, it is possible to bring up abstracts of the articles on the screen to see if they indeed cover the topics of interest. Abstracts and references of relevant articles can then be copied on your printer if you have one, or Dialog will print out the results of any search you do and mail it to you. The printer used by Dialog is fast, and produces very readable output. It generally takes no more than a few days to receive printouts.

Dialog is not cheap. Connect time charges depend on the data base used, but range around $50 per hour. Each *hit* or abstract printed usually costs between 5 and 10 cents. It is possible, however, to save several days in the library reference room by spending 45 minutes on Dialog.

Local Computer Networks

In addition to the nationally available information supermarkets, there are hundreds of local networks run by universities and colleges, computer clubs, amateur radio clubs, and special interest groups. These networks allow a member (or in some cases, anyone who knows the phone number) to call a number and interact with the network's computer. Some systems limit use to reading the local electronic bulletin board, others actually allow access to the programming power of a large computer system from the comfort of your home. Check with your local computer store for information on what is available in your area.

HOW TO BUY A COMMUNICATIONS COMPUTER

A computer must have a set of instructions to follow before it can act as a communications terminal. The term *terminal* refers to any device that can be used to "talk" to a remote computer. You can buy a terminal whose only function is to communicate with the computer, but you probably won't want one.

A terminal program can be obtained in several different ways. Some manufacturers offer an optional cassette that contains the program, while other manufacturers offer the program on either disk or ROM cartridge. The cost of these packages vary between $15 and $400, depending on the sophistication. The more sophisticated a program you have, the more interaction you can have with the remote computer.

Display Characteristics—Every major small computer available today uses either a television or a video monitor as a display screen. The format computers use to display information on the screen, however, varies considerably. For example, some computers can display 24 lines of 40 characters each. That is a total of 960 characters on the screen at one time. Other computers in the under $1000 range also use the 24 by 40 format, 16 lines of 62 characters or 16 lines of 32 characters. More expensive computers generally display 24 lines of 80 characters.

In principle, the more characters on the screen at once the easier it is to use the computer. There are some catches, though. Some computers can display in color and are designed to be used with standard color television. Many, if not most, ordinary televisions make a mess of displaying 24 lines of 80 characters. They are fuzzy and difficult to read. The option then is to have fewer characters on the screen at one time and thus be able to use a regular television or increase the cost of the system and include a color monitor.

Since good color monitors run around $400, many manufacturers have elected to keep the cost of their product down and offer display patterns that can be handled by a television set. Most of the more popular network systems will work nicely with a computer that puts 24 lines of 40 characters on the screen. Some, particularly business and university time-sharing systems, may insist on sending everything to you in 80 character lines. However, many of these will allow you to specify the number of characters you want to display. You should be sure your *host* computer is that agreeable before buying a particular computer for communications. All of the common large data bases such as The Source or CompuServe will let you specify the display width.

Display Options—A second factor to consider is the type of material that can be displayed on the screen. Some computers handle only upper-case letters; others accept both upper- and lower-case; still others accept upper- and lower-case letters as well as many different types of graphic symbols. If your computer is limited, it will limit your access to some networks. When the price is the same, buy the computer with the most display options.

Serial Interface—The actual connection between the computer and the network is via a *serial I/O* port. Just what that cryptic phrase means is explained in Chapter 10. For now, it is only important to know that a computer must have a serial output port to function as a communications computer. Some computers, such as the Osborne I, come with a serial port as standard equipment. Others offer it as an option which can be purchased if needed. Many printers also connect to the computer through the serial port. When a salesperson says a computer has a serial port ask three questions:

1. What baud rates will it accept?
2. Will it run full duplex?
3. Can it function in an auto answer mode?

Here is what those questions mean. The *baud rate* is the speed at which the computer can send and receive information through the serial port. A rate of 300 baud corresponds to a little less than 30 characters per second. Most networks are designed to receive and transmit data at 300 baud, but some can run at 1200 baud (four times as fast). Connections that involve using ordinary long distance phone circuits generally use 300 baud. As you might expect, it is essential that the computer be able to handle 300 baud and it would be nice if it accepted other speeds as well. (Printers that are connected to the serial ports may run as slow as 60 and as high as 1200 baud.)

Now what about the term "full duplex"? Some systems require that the computers on each end of the network take turns. That is, when one is talking the other can only listen. The connection doesn't allow a computer to talk and listen at the same time. That is called *half duplex*. When using a system that is half duplex you have to wait until the computer on the other end finishes sending before you can talk to it. While that may seem like a polite and civilized way to talk to a computer, it can actually lead to problems. Suppose you mistakenly give the computer you're connected to an instruction that causes it to start doing something that may take hours to do (e.g., listing the train schedules for Italy and Yugoslavia) when you really wanted something else (e.g., the schedule for the Milan to Belgrade express). It would be nice to be able to let the computer know you really don't want everything it is dutifully sending you. Look for a computer that can handle *full duplex* communication. At a minimum, the computer should be capable of sending a true BREAK signal out the serial port.

BREAK is a signal many systems use to tell the computer on the other end to stop whatever it is doing and wait for further instructions. Technically, a true BREAK signal involves sending a +5 volt signal to the modem for just under half a second. We have one $4000 computer that has a break key displayed prominently on its keyboard and a fancy set of programs that supposedly turn it into a super-smart terminal. Unfortunately, the programmer and designers forgot to program the break key to send a BREAK signal, and the computer is useless as a terminal unless you modify it. There are several computers that have break keys but no BREAK signal.

Finally, let's deal with *auto answer*. This is really a luxury rather than a requirement, but it is a nice luxury. The standard way to connect to a network is to dial the correct number and listen for a high pitched tone that signals the network is ready to receive data. The phone is then placed in two sponge rubber cups on top of the modem and the connection is made. Then you can type instructions on your keyboard and a computer thousands of miles away will understand and follow them.

When you call another computer and it puts the high pitched tone on the phone line, it is working in an *auto answer mode*. That is, the computer answers the phone and sets up to receive instructions without requiring human assistance. Should you want to be able to call and talk to your computer from a remote location or use it to run a local network for a local club or interest group you will need the auto answer capability.

The Modem—A modem (short for *modulator/demodulator*) converts the electrical signals from the computer into tones which are then transmitted over ordinary phone lines. On the other end another modem converts the tones it hears back into electrical signals the computer can understand. A few years ago it was possible to buy a used modem for as little as $50, but as more and more computer owners learned about all the nice things you can do with a modem, the used equipment was quickly snapped up.

There are still kits that provide you with all the parts needed for a modem. Unless you have experience building with integrated circuits and soldering tiny, heat sensitive parts on a circuit board we advise you to buy an assembled unit. That advice is particularly valid these days because several inex-

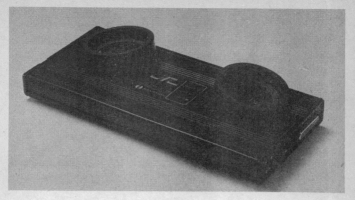

Modem

pensive modems are now available. Several manufacturers sell modems for prices between $150 and $275. But all modems are not created equal. A modem can be a half duplex or full duplex model. You want a full duplex modem because it can be switched to half duplex when required.

Modems can also be *answer*, *originate*, or *answer and originate*. These terms require a little explaining. When an answer modem is told to send a *1* out, it sends a 2225 Hz tone; it sends a 2025 Hz tone when it is told to send a *0*. Each letter and number has a code, much like the telegrapher's Morse code, with 1's and 0's replacing the dits and dahs. The code for a capital A for example is 1000001. A modem converts this code into a pattern of tones to transmit them over the phone. There is, however, a slight twist in the plot. Answer modems transmit tones in the 2000 Hz range, but they do not receive tones in that range. They *listen* for two tones—a 1270 Hz tone that stands for a 1 and a 1070 Hz tone that stands for a 0. The different receive and transmit tones are necessary to keep the modem from receiving its own transmissions.

Now what about the originate modems? As you might expect, they receive the tones that answer modems transmit and transmit the tones answer modems receive. Thus two answer or two originate modems can't talk to each other. If you have a friend in Pocatello, with an ATARI computer, your computers can only talk to each other if one has an answer modem and the other has an originate.

Most networks have an answer modem so you should at least get an originate modem. The best option, however, is to get a modem that can be used in either answer or originate modes. They cost more, but they are much more versatile. The ATARI modem has a switch that allows you to change from answer to originate.

One final comment about modems. They are rated according to the highest speed (baud rate) which can be used with them. Almost all the modems used on small computers are rated up to 300 baud. Commercial modems that reliably transmit and receive at very high baud rates are also very expensive. Buy one only if you really need the capability.

CHAPTER 6

The Teaching Machine

The term "revolution" is frequently used to describe the past ten years in computer technology. Like many other high-impact or superlative words, "revolution" may be used more often today than the facts justify. Still, what has happened to computers since 1972 probably has as much right to be called a revolution as anything else during the period. We recently heard someone suggest that there is, or soon will be, a revolution in education, too. In the near future, computers will become a standard piece of equipment in the classroom.

We do not believe there is now, nor is there soon likely to be, a revolution in the little red schoolhouse. The best we can hope for is fast evolution. Education has never been known for its willingness to embrace new technology (some suggest we are still trying to deal with the printing press and moveable-type). And when education has accepted technology, the promises made by the technocrats have rarely, if ever, been fulfilled. Educational television is a good example from our recent past. It did not revolutionize education as promised, but it is a tool that is sometimes useful for accomplishing some educational goals.

Many experienced teachers can list at least ten "new" ideas or new technologies that were supposed to revolutionize education. Yet teachers still teach in much the same way they did 30 years ago. You can understand why educators aren't rushing to embrace new computer technology.

In spite of the reasons why we won't see a revolution in education, there is good reason to expect that education will evolve or change rather quickly during the next ten years. We feel there are two main thrusts that will bring more change in the next decade than has occurred in the last 50 years.

THE DESCHOOLING OF LEARNING

For most of the twentieth century, education has been institutionalized. Learning is something children do in a classroom supervised by one or more adults. The traditional school will not disappear, but before the end of this century it will likely play a much smaller role in learning than it does today. More people will spend a significant amount of time learning at home, in the office, the factory, and at adult learning centers. Increasingly, our society is viewing learning as a lifelong task rather than something children do to prepare for adulthood. That view is being accepted today because we live in a time of accelerated change. Information is outdated quickly; and new information seems to appear at a faster and faster rate. Secretaries must learn to deal with *word processors*, office machine repair personnel must deal with electronic calculators instead of mechanical ones, and factory workers have to learn about industrial robots. It's hard to find the mainspring in a digital watch and even more difficult to find the pilot light on a microwave oven.

The point is that we must continue to learn, regardless of our age, if we are to cope with the demands of life today, and that learning must occur someplace other than the classrooms where we spent the fourth grade. Fortunately, the small computer came along at a time when it can be particularly helpful in both traditional and non-traditional learning environments.

THE SMALL COMPUTER AS A LEARNING MACHINE

Computers have been used in education for at least 20 years. Pioneering projects such as Suppes' work at Stanford University, however, used large, expensive computers which could not be placed in individual classrooms or resource centers. Instead, a keyboard/printer device called a *terminal* was placed in the school and connected to the computer by phone. This method was the only option available 15 years ago, and it is still a major means of getting computer-based learning into the classroom. Control Data's PLATO project is a sophisticated system of computer-assisted learning capable of teaching everything from pre-school letter recognition to graduate level physics. Another commercial venture, Computer Curriculum Corporation, uses large computers to distribute their educational programs to several hundred school systems.

In spite of the history of large computers as learning machines, we feel the future of educational computing lies in the increased use of small computers. They are cheaper, easier to use, more reliable, and easier to install in a school. When faced with the choice of buying one large computer or 100 small computers, school districts are now frequently electing to buy small computers such as the ATARI 400 or 800, the Apple II, the PET, the Texas Instruments 99/4A, and the TRS-80 Model III. The small computers often cost far less than the price of a terminal for one of the larger systems.

Dependability is probably the second major reason schools are buying small computers. To use a time-sharing system requires a terminal that is working, a phone line that is reasonably clear of interference, and a remotely located computer (sometimes several hundred miles away) that is not only working but has the time to respond quickly to the student at the terminal. If any one of the elements in the chain isn't working, the entire system doesn't work and a scheduled learning period in the classroom is lost. The logistics of using small computers are much less involved and therefore inherently more reliable.

Microcomputers in a classroom

A distinguished computer educator put the point very clearly
in a recent article:

> The inexpensive microcomputer, more than any other event,
> has made school-based computer education a possibility. The
> development of small time-sharing systems about ten years ago
> brought hardware costs per student terminal down to about
> $10,000—a major breakthrough, but still far too costly for
> most schools. Worse yet, time-sharing systems lack robustness
> against hardware failure: 97% uptime is achievable and sounds
> good, but it means that there is no computer one day per month,
> and no computer class. The new personal computers have brought
> the cost down from $10,000 to $2000 and have increased ro-
> bustness dramatically: 97% uptime for personal computers means
> that out of a collection of ten machines, nine are working all
> the time and all ten are working most of the time. Class goes
> on. (A. Luehrmann, "Computer Illiteracy—A National Crisis
> and a Solution for It," *Byte*, July, 1980, pp. 98–102)

Don't expect to see 35 small computers in your daughter's
fifth grade classroom next year (although you might), but the
use of computers in traditional educational settings will in-

crease tremendously in the next five years. Educational computing will grow at an even faster rate in home and office settings. Some companies appear to have made a corporate decision that their learning products will be purchased in larger quantities by parents than by schools. Products such as *Speak and Spell*, *Speak and Read*, and *Magic Wand* have all been marketed very successfully to parents. Although such handheld learning aids are excellent educational tools, schools have accounted for only a small fraction of their sales. If you are interested in learning more about computer-aided learning you may want to read current issues of the three computer-oriented education magazines listed below:

The Computing Teacher (Computing Center, Eastern Oregon State College, La Grande, Oregon 97850). One of the oldest publications in the field, it carries a range of articles on the use of computers in elementary and secondary schools.

Educational Computer Magazine (P.O. Box 535, Cupertino, California 95015). Begun in 1981, this is a user-oriented magazine designed primarily for educators who want to use computers in their schools. If early issues are any indication it will be a very good publication.

Classroom Computer News (P.O. Box 266, Cambridge, Massachusetts 02138). Also begun in 1981, this publication uses a modified newspaper format and covers some of the same areas as *Educational Computer Magazine*. Publishes a directory of educational computing resources. Well worth the price of a subscription.

Books of interest include *The Computer in the School: Tutor, Tool, Tutee* (Columbia University Press, 1981), edited by Robert P. Taylor. This book consists of a very good introductory chapter and reprints of articles by pioneers Alfred Bork, Thomas Dwyer, Arthur Luehrmann, Seymour Papert, and Patrick Suppes. Another book we recommend is *Computers, Teaching and Learning* by Willis, Johnson, and Dixon. Their book, available from dilithium Press, is an introduction to educational computing. Another excellent book on educational computing is *Practical Guide to Computers in Education*, published by Addison-Wesley.

WHAT CAN COMPUTERS DO?

The focus of this section will be on what computers *can* do rather than what they *are* doing at present. Currently most public school students and many university students have no contact at all with a computer during their educational career. In relation to education the computer can be viewed in two general ways: as the focus of learning and as an aid to the learning process. The first view is embodied in the concept of "computer literacy." Arthur Luehrmann, in an article in *Byte* (July, 1980, pp. 98–102) made this observation:

> Computing plays such a crucial role in everyday life and in the technological future of this nation that the general public's ignorance of the subject constitutes a national crisis.
>
> The ability to use computers is as basic and necessary to a person's formal education as reading, writing, and arithmetic. . . .
>
> Yet, despite computing's critical importance today, the overwhelming majority of this country's general public is woefully ill-prepared to live and work in the Age of Information as some have called it.

Luehrmann makes the point many people are making these days: those of the next generation are going to have a hard time doing their jobs if they don't understand computers and how they are used. Even if computers could not be used to teach reading, math, and the other school subjects, they would be important as a topic of study themselves. Several computer manufacturers have gone to considerable lengths to provide books, computer-aided learning programs, and audio-visual aids in the area of computer literacy. Tandy, the manufacturer of the TRS-80 computer, has several training packages which can be used by teachers offering courses on computer literacy. Apple and Atari also have materials which can be used in the classroom or at home to learn about computers and their use. In addition, a variety of publishers are publishing both educational software and computer literacy books.

The second view of computers in education—the computer as an aid to learning other subjects—is, in our view, just as important as computer literacy. The computer, particularly the small computer, offers both educators and learners unique features that help both deal with the demands of an information-oriented society.

As mentioned earlier, computers have been used in education for many years. Early efforts grew out of the work of mechanical teaching machines and programmed learning—two movements that gained strength in the late 50s and early 60s and then subsided as problems and difficulties in application overwhelmed early hopes for the new methods. Computers were seen as one way to get around some of the problems of machines and programmed texts. Many programmed instruction books were boring. In addition, it was difficult to individualize instruction. Even if a student understood something the first time it was presented, the lesson might keep presenting it over and over. Or, if a student needed additional instruction to reinforce learning, the programmed instruction lesson might go on to new material. Early computer-assisted instruction did solve some problems, but it created new ones (e.g., reliability and costs) and was never accepted or used by even a large minority of the teachers and professors.

Reliability and cost factors are no longer the problems they were then. Small computers that run most of the time and cost less than $1000 have attracted the interest of many school systems. There are even a few major educational computing efforts at the state or provincial level. Funded by a forward-looking legislature, the Minnesota Educational Computing Consortium is one of the oldest and most successful projects. MECC began with the idea of using a large time-sharing computer that would be accessed from schools over phone lines. In recent years, however, their focus has shifted to the use of small computers. Some of MECC's educational software is now marketed nationally. Other projects using small computers are underway in Alaska, Texas, British Columbia, and many other areas.

Computers are being used to teach basic academic skills as well as art, music, and creative writing. There is even a special language called PILOT which was designed specifically for educational computing.

Computer-Assisted Instruction (CAI), Computer-Aided Instruction (CAI), and Computer-Assisted Learning (CAL) are all terms in general use that refer to the use of a computer in education. Although some authors have tried to give specific meanings to each term they are usually used interchangeably. Several more terms such as Computer-Managed Instruction (CMI), Drill and Practice (D&P), and Simulation refer to specific types of computer-aided learning. In this section of the chapter we will provide some definitions of these terms and give examples of programs that aid learning.

Drill and Practice

The simplest type of computer-assisted instruction is drill and practice. D&P doesn't really teach you anything, it just gives you practice in something you learned in some other way. A common D&P program would be one that gives the student practice in using basic math skills. A crude program for addition, for example, would randomly select two numbers to be added, display the problem on the screen, and wait for the student to type in an answer. If the answer is correct another problem is presented; an incorrect answer usually means the computer will ask the student to try again. Two errors in a row means the student is given the answer. The computer then continues to give problems to be solved.

A more sophisticated type of drill and practice program that teaches touch typing is available from several companies. Most computers can run at least one version of the program. The better versions have several levels of practice and a number of sophisticated features. The beginning levels give the student practice on individual letters which are presented in groups of five or so. For a total beginner, several of the programs start by drilling on typing **A S D F** and **G**, the *home* keys for the left hand.

The beginner progresses through all the letters, numbers, and punctuation symbols on the keyboard and then begins to type words or letter groups followed by sentences and paragraphs. The program keeps track of errors and identifies characters a student has trouble with; it times work and prints out a speed in words per minute after an exercise. One version puts a color-coded display of the keyboard on the screen while the student gets started. If a word is left out during an exercise, the color of the word missed is changed. As the student becomes more

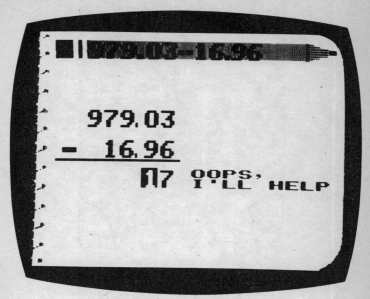

Drill and practice

proficient, the computer remembers troublesome words or letters and gives more practice on them. It is a friendly, convenient, effective way to learn touch typing.

Even fancier drill and practice programs select the difficulty level of problems on the basis of the student's performance during earlier sessions; they remember errors and give the student extra practice. If used in a school setting they may provide the teacher with printouts of individual student and class progress. A well-known educational publisher, SRA (155 N. Wacker Drive, Chicago, Illinois 60606) markets a line of educational software packages that includes drill and practice programs for addition, subtraction, multiplication, and division facts. When teachers and students use these programs, the type and beginning difficulty level of problems can be selected by the teacher or the student. Once begun, the computer keeps track of the student's performance and moves on to more difficult problems when the student masters the current level.

Drill and practice

Drills can be timed if desired so that students try to "beat the clock" and still get the correct answer. The programs keep track of students' performance and provide a printed record for the teacher.

There are also several interesting games which the students get to play if they do well on their exercise. SRA's material is a bit more than a drill and practice program. For example, it uses the graphics features of the computer to provide several types of "help" to students who don't quite understand how to do a problem.

SRA also has a program called *Phonics* which is designed to be used in conjunction with a basal reading program for students in the primary grades.

In the coming months and years, there are likely to be thousands of drill and practice programs available on a wide range of topics.

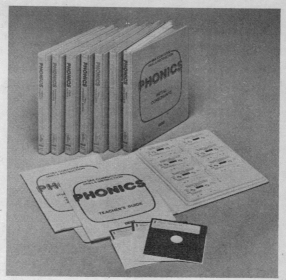

SRA Phonics program

Tutorial Programs

A tutorial program does more than just give you practice on something you already know. It actually teaches. At the college level, the organization Conduit (Box 388, Iowa City, Iowa 52244) distributes a number of educational programs that run on small computers. There are programs that teach a student to apply Newton's Second Law and the Law of Gravitation to satellite orbits and another that teaches matrix algebra.

At the high school and college level there is a large selection of tutorial programs for small computers. Subjects covered include U.S. history, accounting, psychology, physics, algebra, supervisory skills, counseling procedures, sociology, and business communications. There are also a number of programs that teach conversational French, Spanish, German, or Italian.

Educational computing programs that use a tutorial format rather than a drill and practice method are much more difficult to write, since you must teach the skill as well as evaluate learning. The number of tutorial programs available is not likely to increase quickly, but there are indications that a number of traditional educational publishers are preparing tutorial software for many of the required subjects at the elementary and high school level.

A computer tutorial

Simulations

We have a program called *Oregon Trail* that grabs the attention of both adults and children when it is used as a demonstration. *Oregon Trail* tells the group around the computer that they are on a wagon train leaving St. Joseph, Missouri, for Oregon. The program allows the group to make decisions on how much food, bullets, medicine, and clothing to buy. They then select a wagon and oxen team, pay for them, and head for Oregon. Along the way the wagon train can run into all sorts of problems—floods, hostile raiders, blizzards, broken wagons, and sickness. The settlers must decide how much food to eat each day, when to hunt, what to do when raiders appear, and whether to stop and buy provisions at the forts along the way.

The decisions made determine the likelihood of different types of problems occurring (e.g., eat poorly and you are more likely to become ill). While we have buried many a group of settlers along the trail to Oregon, some groups do make it through.

Oregon Trail is one of many simulations available today. A computer simulation puts the participant in a role and then requires decisions that have consequences. Most computers have a version of a simulation called *Hammurabi* that makes the player the ruler of an ancient city which has 1000 acres of land for cultivation, 100 citizens, and 3000 bushels of grain in storage. As ruler you must decide how much grain to give the people to eat, how much to save for seed, and how many acres to plant. Your decisions determine whether the kingdom starves or grows and develops (and requires more grain next year).

Another popular simulation is marketed under several names. It puts you in charge of a large nuclear power plant and requires you to run it successfully without an accident. This simulation is actually quite realistic and teaches the fundamentals of nuclear power in an enjoyable format.

Simulations are widely used in business and industry. Nuclear and chemical plant workers are trained by computer simulations. It is much less expensive to have a trainee blow up a make-believe plant on the screen than to make a real mistake while training in a real plant. Simulations are not only effective training tools, they are also fun. Many of the computer and arcade games that are so popular today are simulations designed for maximum enjoyment rather than as learning aids.

Other Educational Applications

Computer literacy, drill and practice, tutorial programs, and simulations account for the great majority of computer applications in education today. Another approach, Computer-Managed Learning (CML), uses the computer as a manager or overseer of learning. For example, students may be given a series of assignments that require them to read certain sections of a text and do some work in the library. As the student finishes each assignment he or she sits down at the computer and takes a test over the assignment. A pass means the student can go on to the next assignment, otherwise the computer provides suggestions for further study. CML requires quite a bit of work for the teacher to arrange, but does not require the teacher to actually write programs that teach the student. In addition, CML makes sense when computer presentation of the material is not feasible or not efficient (i.e., in a class on Old English poetry). The computer can still be used as an aid to learning even if it does not actually do the teaching.

In the future, computers may be used to identify the academic weaknesses of students through extensive diagnostic testing and to prescribe educational programs to meet a particular student's needs. They may also come to be considered useful tools in many classes, much as calculators have. In addition, the small computer holds great promise as an aid to physically handicapped students. Computers are already being used as communications devices by students who cannot speak. The future looks bright for educational computing whether it be in traditional classrooms or in a non-traditional setting such as the home.

Chapter 9 on business applications is also relevant to educational computing since many computers in schools play important roles as business computers. The same computer that is used in a typing or word processing class can be used in a class on accounting or business. It may also be used in the school's office to keep the books and to maintain pupil records. Addison-Wesley, Scott Foresman, and SRA all have accounting and record keeping software designed specifically for the school market.

SELECTING AN EDUCATIONAL COMPUTER

Although most of the personal computers available today can be used as learning aids there are some features which are more important in a learning environment than they are in other settings. Chapter 3 is a detailed guide to buying a personal computer. You should probably consider this section as a sort of supplement to Chapter 3 which deals with the most important questions to ask before buying an educational computer for the school or home.

Is It Easy to Learn to Use?

Computers in schools are used by many different students and often by many different teachers as well. If there is too much *learning overhead*, that is, if the computer is so complicated to use that it takes each user five or ten hours to learn to turn the machine on, load a program, and begin using it, the system is not suitable for educational applications.

Computers designed primarily for business applications often require a one- to five-day training program for primary operators. A business can afford such a time investment if there are only a few people who will use the computer, and if there is not a high staff turnover rate. Since there is a new crop of students each semester or year, the educational computer must be relatively easy to learn to use.

Even if the computer will be used in the home for educational purposes, its operation should be simple enough that younger children in the family can operate it independently.

Is the Computer "Friendly"?

Many people approach a computer with considerable trepidation and anxiety. Even if the computer is relatively easy to use, the anxious operator who expects it to be difficult to use will find that it is. The design of the computer should be such that a new user feels fairly comfortable using it. An attractive case, simple but functional keyboard, use of color coding, and absence of any *doomsday* keys all contribute to a friendly computer. A doomsday key is one that, when pressed by accident, will destroy the program in the computer's memory. There are few things worse for a first-time computer user than being told, "Whatever you do, don't hit this key; if you do it will destroy everything in memory!" The anxious learner often spends more time in trying to stay away from that key than in learning to use the computer (and it is, of course, the first key the curious learner pushes).

Computer programs can also have doomsday instructions in them. Some word processing programs have instructions that delete everything you have typed into the computer's memory. A student who has just spent six hours of hard work typing in a term paper will be understandably upset if he or she inadvertently hits a key that erases everything before it is printed. A *friendly* word processing program will make it difficult to erase large amounts of material (e.g., require pressing several keys at once rather than one or two) or will ask, "Are you sure?" before doing something drastic.

What Kind of Input Options Are Available?

Some computers will only permit you to talk to them through the keyboard. That is convenient for some purposes and inefficient for others. Educational programs can often take advantage of other input options such as joysticks and light pens.

A light pen is a small device shaped much like a ball point pen. When placed against the television screen the computer can "read" its signal and determine where it is located. An educational program that involves multiple choice items, for example, could use a light pen instead of the keyboard for input. When choosing an answer, the student only has to put the tip of the light pen beside the selection.

What Kind of Output Options Are Available?

Virtually any computer will display letters and numbers on the screen, but some are capable of generating complicated sound output and very sophisticated color graphics as well as text. The interest and sophistication of some educational programs are enhanced by sound and by good color graphics. It is one thing to read about how a gasoline engine works; it is something entirely different to watch an animated model of an engine appear on the screen and go through each of its cycles. Not only is the display more interesting than the text, it can actually teach many concepts far better than simple text.

Is It Kid Proof?

No electronic equipment is completely immune from prying hands and inquisitive minds, but an educational computer should be designed so that a child cannot easily damage it or be damaged by it. Recently we saw an electronic cash register completely destroyed in a cafeteria when a customer accidentally spilled a large cup of coffee onto the keyboard while reaching for change in his pocket. The cash register's keyboard was a standard *open* type with a circuit board located just under the keys. The coffee shorted out the machine and did so much damage that the cash register had to be junked.

Many computers have keyboards with circuits just under them. They are more likely to be damaged by a liquid spilled on the keyboard than computers such as the Sinclair ZX81, which uses a *membrane* keyboard. Membrane keyboards are usually made of one piece of embossed plastic that does not allow anything to get between the keys and into the computer itself.

Some computers also present a significant hazard to children because high voltages are present at locations which are easy to get to. Several popular systems with removable tops or cases, for example, have a potentially lethal 120 volts at several unprotected locations. An educational computer should not be too easy to disassemble. If using the computer does require removal of part of the cover or case, access should not expose the user to lethal voltages. Bell and Howell, a major supplier of educational products, sells a special version of the Apple II computer that has been "kid proofed." Its top is firmly screwed down and the connectors on the back have been modified to take rough use.

Another aspect of kid proofing is the way accessories are connected to the computer. Connectors should be clearly labeled, and there should be little or no likelihood of connecting something to the wrong plug. Some systems, for example, use the same type of connector for the power cord and the accessories. Accidentally plugging the power cord into the wrong socket can produce a variety of unwanted fireworks. To summarize, an educational computer should be safe and protected from accident and likely human errors.

Is There a Special Pricing Arrangement? What Kind of Service Is Available?

Several computer manufacturers, recognizing the importance of educational computing, offer schools a special price break. As this chapter was written Commodore, Radio Shack and Atari were all offering an "educational discount" to schools. Texas Instruments and Apple do not have across-the-board discounts to schools, but both have provided significant amounts of equipment to selected schools and Apple has a national bid department that will bid well below the retail price of the computers on larger orders even if they are pooled across several school systems. Apple also provides school systems who buy their first Apple computer with a package of books and software which can be used in computer literacy classes and in teacher training programs. Virtually all the major manufacturers are involved in at least a few demonstration projects.

Service, which was discussed in Chapter 3, is particularly important in educational settings. Class meets whether the computer is working or not, thus dependability and service are important.

Can Networking Capabilities Be Added If Required?

Radio Shack offers a $500 device that allows a teacher to load one program into a central computer and to simultaneously load the program into the computers being used by the students as well. This feature, called *networking*, is not useful for home applications, but it is very helpful in computer classes which involve many students working on the same program each day. The time required to individually load a program into 25 different computers can be considerable. Nestar Corporation offers a system called *Cluster One* that allows a school system to interconnect as many as 65 Apple II computers located within 1000 feet of each other. Cluster One has several very sophisticated features which are handy for business as well as school applications. As you might expect, Cluster One's price is high. Other, less expensive, downloading systems are available for most popular small computers. The Commodore computers, in fact, are capable of networking with a minimum of extra equipment.

What Software Is Available

It goes without saying that you must have educational software to have an educational computer. Lack of available software, in fact, has been one of the major reasons why computers are not more common in classrooms. If you have a particular application in mind, be sure the computer you buy has software for that application. Several computers, Apple II, the TRS-80 Model III, the ATARI computers, and the Commodore computers all have a substantial amount of educational software written for them. The Texas Instruments computer also has quite a bit of educational software available, especially at the elementary and pre-school level. Many less popular computers simply have not attracted the attention required to induce educational publishers and software writers to develop programs for them.

SUMMARY

In addition to the general considerations discussed in Chapter 3, purchasers of a computer to be used for educational purposes should look for the following features:

1. Ease of use for beginners.

2. User friendliness—does not intimidate first time users, has no doomsday features.

3. Multiple input options—has provisions for accessories such as light pens, game paddles and joysticks.

4. Output options—offers color displays, graphics and sound.

5. Kid proofing—does not present a danger to young and curious users, and is not easy to damage by accident or human error.

6. Special pricing—if available, so much the better; but service availability is more important.

7. Networking—if this is a requirement, check on both availability and cost.

8. Software—has high-quality programs available.

CHAPTER 7

The Working Computer

In this chapter, we will discuss both kinds of working computers: the business computer and the managerial computer. A business computer will help you manage your day-to-day business operations efficiently. Various computer industry experts estimate that nearly one-third of all small computers sold are used by managers. These estimates range from 100,000 a year to "half of what Apple sells." Whatever the number, the important thing is that managers are buying and using a lot of small computers. Why? To answer this question we will start with a discussion of managerial uses of computers. We aren't going to forget small businesses though, so we will finish the chapter with small business applications and a guide to buying a business computer.

MANAGERIAL USES OF SMALL COMPUTERS

In the future, how well you use a computer may determine how successful you are in your work. You are probably familiar with the old adage, "Genius is 90 percent perspiration and 10 percent inspiration." A computer can't do anything about the 10 percent but it sure can make the 90 percent a lot easier. No matter what your profession, you spend a large portion of your time doing humdrum chores. A computer can help relieve the humdrum and give you more time to be a genius. If you use it only to write letters and compute cash flow, your computer will probably pay for itself in short order.

Word Processing

We will start with that boon to secretaries and writers—the word processor. If you write anything—letters, reports, articles, books—word processing can be a big time saver. For example, have you ever written a letter, had it typed, and then found something you wanted to change? With a typewriter it usually means typing the entire letter over and reproofing everything. With a word processor, making a change is a minor adjustment and after you have made the change you can print out a letter-perfect copy. Word processors let you store a copy of the letter on cassette or diskette and reuse it. Changes involve no more than loading the letter back into the computer's memory (from the diskette or cassette), making your changes, and printing another copy. The same procedure is used to revise and update reports, articles, and chapters of books.

Financial Modeling

Even if you don't use a computer for word processing, accounting or inventory control, there are still excellent reasons for using one. We can only cover just a few of the managerial applications of small computers, but there are several good books available on this subject. For instance, Dartnell has published an excellent book on the managerial uses of small computers entitled *The Manager's Desktop Computer*, by Nicholas Rosa and Merl Miller.

For years, financial analysts and economists have used mainframes and expensive time-sharing systems to predict corporate and national economic performance. Financial modeling—a partial simulation of real or possible situations—has assumed an aura of the mysterious for many managers. How-

VisiCalc worksheet

ever, modern financial modeling tools, high speed computers, and sophisticated software are now within the reach of anyone.

More than 15 programs, ranging in price from $80 to $1500, perform basic financial modeling and analysis on a variety of machines. Of course, the program's power and capabilities vary with cost, but you can find personal computer software that will let you perform financial modeling at a fraction of the cost of a larger system.

What is financial modeling software? Simply put, a model of any kind is a small copy of the real thing. A sophisticated financial modeling package is a tool which allows you to simulate the future on paper. It helps you evaluate future actions. Computerized financial models let you very quickly analyze the possible effects of different actions. Models do this through mathematical equations. These equations can easily be drafted as a computer program or a set of rules that a computer can process.

Financial models can also be used to look backward and analyze a company's past performance. They can help you discover where problems occurred and why.

The less expensive microcomputer-based programs do not have the sophistication or power of the major time-sharing systems. However, if you are not an accountant or a financial manager, a small computer program will probably fit or exceed your needs. Even if you are an accountant or financial manager, you may find that one of these programs will do most of your work. For everything you give up in power and sophistication, you get back twice as much in convenience. A desktop computer will let you make as many changes as you want at no extra cost.

Microcomputer-based financial models can be divided into three categories according to their features and limitations. However, despite their different terminologies, all are based on the intersections of rows of columns within electronic spread sheets. They perform calculations using formulas, or rules inserted into row and column intersections. In the top category are those programs most similar to the time-sharing programs, *RCS*, *FPL* and *MINIMODEL*. These programs are followed by *VisiCalc*, *SuperCalc*, *Decision Evaluator System*, *Desktop Plan*, *Target*, *T-MARKER*, *PLANNER PLUS* and *EXECU-PLAN*. The last category would include *REPORT WRITER*, *COL-U-PAD D* and *FINPLAN*.

The best selling program is *VisiCalc*. It is priced reasonably and it may be all you need. Its closest competitor is *SuperCalc*. Figure 7.1 is an example of a *SuperCalc* worksheet. You can enter data everywhere you want on the worksheet and then manipulate it. The program will repeat numbers, text or formulas. The real secret of a spreadsheet program is *recalculation*. If you change one number on the worksheet, all related numbers change automatically. This lets you ask all kinds of "what if" questions easily and quickly.

As an example of how you can use a spread sheet, let's look at cash flow. Cash flow has become a major concern for managers of both small businesses and departments of large businesses. Cash flow can be very complicated and the exact cash flow requirements vary from business to business. Here are some general factors that need to be considered when you are doing a cash flow analysis (you may want to add a few of your own):

	A	C	D	E	F
70					
71	BALANCE SHEET AS OF	9-30-79	9-30-80	9-30-81	3-31-82
72					
73					
74	ASSETS				
75	CASH	23067	18762	22910	1032
76	ACCTS RECVBLE	71170	14411	319105	412673
77	INVENTORY	82943	142164	212913	196188
78	ROYALTY ADVANCES	0	0	33323	50365
79	PREPAID EXPENSES	3429	14521	11164	8671
80	NOTES RECEIVABLE	0	6128	0	0
81	EQUIPMENT	0	0	165147	184786
82	ACCUMLTD DEPR.	0	0	-17783	-34419
83	NET EQUIPMENT	0	0	147364	150367
84	COPYRIGHTS	0	0	10000	13421
85	ACCUMLTD AMORT.	0	0	-1430	-1430
86	OTHER ASSETS	0	0	8570	11991
87					
88	TOTAL ASSETS	180609	195986	755349	831287

Figure 7.1. A sample SuperCalc worksheet

Cash

1. What percentage of your customers pay cash?
2. Do you accept credit cards? What is the discount schedule on the credit cards you accept?
3. What is your loss from bad checks?
4. Do you give a discount for cash with order?

Accounts Receivable

1. What percentage of the accounts receivable falls into the various aging categories. For example, you may have 20 percent that are less than 30 days, 30 percent that are 30 to 60 days, 30 percent that are 60 to 90 days, and 20 percent that are over 90 days.
2. Is your business seasonal?
3. What is the payment history of your customers? Has it changed in the last six months or year?
4. What is the general payment pattern in your industry?
5. Do you give a discount for payment within 10 days?

Accounts Payable

1. Is there a discount for early payment?
2. How often do you make payments?
3. Do any of your suppliers charge interest?
4. Can you make partial payments when necessary?

Sales

1. Are your sales projections accurate?
2. Are sales made to the same customers or are new customers constantly being added and old customers being dropped?
3. What are your terms?

General Overhead

1. What are your fixed expenses?
2. Is your payroll fixed or variable?
3. Can some of your fixed expenses be paid quarterly rather than monthly?

Banking

1. At what rate do you borrow money?
2. Can you increase revenue by using savings accounts?

You probably do something like this now. If you are not using a computer, you probably take many hours and sometimes you are still off by quite a bit. With a computer, not only can you make more accurate forecasts, but you can also experiment with a wide variety of scenarios. Most managers like to think through, "What would happen if. . . ." Your computer can give you this capability.

One of the key elements of the cash flow projection is the sales forecast. This projection is usually made by the sales or marketing manager. If you are a sales manager, your real interest is people, not a bunch of numbers on a piece of paper. Most sales managers think of sales projections as absolute drudgery. But forecasts are part of the job, so you do them.

Well, we have some good news and some bad news. The bad news is you are still going to have to make out reports and do forecasts. The good news is your computer will make it easier. Think about this: isn't most of what you project based on educated guessing? Obviously, a computer can handle numbers; all you have to do is tell it which ones.

OTHER PROFESSIONAL USES OF COMPUTERS

Perhaps you are not a manager, but you would like to be one. What can a computer do for you? First of all, you can use it for everything your manager does. Not only will you be able to produce better reports, but you will be gaining some valuable experience. If you are a sales representative, you can keep your tickler file on your computer. (A tickler file is a list of customers, along with some pertinent information about each one.) You can also keep a product file on your computer. For instance, a real estate agent might have a list of current prospects on one diskette and a list of houses on another.

We could describe an almost endless variety of professions and show you how to use a computer to increase productivity in each. We won't do that. We will say, though, that regardless of your profession, there is probably some way you can use a computer to improve the quality of your work and free up more of your time. There are even some ways you can tie into some other people's data bases and use their ideas and information. These applications were explained in Chapter 5, "The Outer Limits."

A SMALL BUSINESS COMPUTER

If you are in business, you need a computer. It is as simple as that. You may think that your business is too small, but if it supports you, it is not too small to benefit from a computer. Every company from the giant corporation to the neighborhood service station or local real estate office can use a computer.

You already know about giant corporate computers, so let's talk about a service station owner. Let's call him Joe. The Down Home Gas and Supply, as Joe calls his station, is a popular place. Joe sells gas at 10 cents above his cost and he only charges $15.00 an hour for mechanical work. Best of all, he is an excellent mechanic. His profits from gas sales cover most of his overhead, but he does have to do some mechanical work to break even. Therefore, his earnings come from his mechanical work and the sale of parts. When he added parts and labor together, his gross profit on mechanical work is about $17.00 an hour.

He spends about 30 hours a month on his books (1 hour a night and 4 to 5 hours extra at month's end). This is 30 hours he could spend doing mechanical work. If he can cut the book-work down to 10 hours a month, he will increase his revenue by $340.00. He can do this with a computer that costs less than $175.00 a month. (This assumes that he buys a computer that costs about $5000.00 and pays for it over a three year period.) At the end of three years, he will own the computer and his expenses will be limited to maintenance.

A computer won't solve all of Joe's problems, but it will help. Not only will it increase his profits by allowing him more time to do mechanical work, it will also help in other areas. For instance, using careful inventory control, he can be sure he has enough of the parts he needs and he can return or sell those he doesn't need. This feature alone can save him enough money to pay for the computer.

How to Buy a Business Computer

When you buy a computer for your business, you are making a major decision. If you haven't done so yet, we suggest that you read Chapter 3 before starting this one. The buying steps we outlined in Chapter 3 can be a very good starting point, so we will briefly review them here.

Step One: Identify your major uses. If you buy a tyepwriter or a truck, you have a specific use in mind. The same should be true when you buy a computer.

Step Two: Specify minimum requirements and preferred features. This is where you get down to the real nitty-gritty. The hardware items you want for sure are 48K of memory and a good printer. The minimum software packages you want are an accounting package and a word processing package. But what else do you need?

Step Three: Identify likely secondary uses and desirable machine features. For instance, you will certainly want to use your computer as a managerial aid. You may want color for this application and you might not see any use for color in your primary application.

Step Four: Decide how much you want to spend—now and later. Are there ways of buying the computer that will save you money? Should you buy outright? Should you rent or lease? If you do buy outright, should you pay cash or should you finance?

Step Five: Survey the field. This is so important for a business computer user that there is no way we can overemphasize it. The microcomputer is an outgrowth of the semiconductor industry, not the computer industry. This is both good and bad.

The good news is that a complete computer system is priced within the reach of any small business. The bad news is that

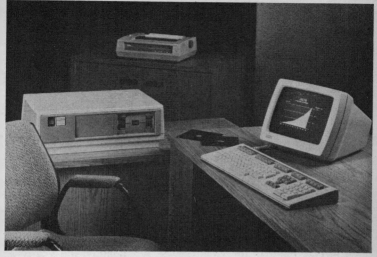

A DEC 325 business computer system

you will have to go through a lot of chaff to get to the wheat. Most small computer companies and computer stores were started by engineers or computer hobbyists. Many of these people are absolute geniuses, but they don't understand business computing at all. Our advice is to be careful and talk to a lot of people. It is not like buying a car.

Step Six: Survey sources. It is probably best to go to an established dealer, but it is not crucial. It depends on your definition of established dealer. Most of the dealers were not even in business five years ago, so judge all of them essentially the same. Find out as much as you can about the people who own and run the store.

Step Seven: Buy it.

Managing Your Three Major Resources

How well you manage your three major resources—time, talent and treasure—will determine how successful you are. A computer should be considered a tool to help optimize the use of one or more of these resources. The real key to buying a business computer is listed in Buying Step One. You have to know what you are going to use the computer for. You should begin your survey by analyzing how you sell your product (or service).

Because the computer is merely a tool, it must have a specific job. If you define this job carefully, your selection process will be a lot easier. There are five key questions you need to ask yourself:

1. What data must I get from the computer?
2. What form should this data be in?
3. How much storage do I need?
4. What is it going to take to input data?
5. What would I like the computer to accomplish?

We will define the term data here, but you don't have to understand the term to understand this process. Data consists of the facts and figures you use in your business. Starting with item one above, the first thing to do is make a list of the data you want from your computer. A sample list for Joe's service station is shown below:

1. Gas pumped on a daily, weekly, monthly and yearly basis.
2. Customer list including home address, phone number and type of car (or cars) and perhaps a maintenance record for each.
3. Inventory of parts carried showing what is selling and what isn't. For instance, do we sell more radial tires than two-plys, and what is the difference in profit margin on these items?
4. Bookkeeping, keeping track of payroll, taxes, sales, etc. Maybe we can come up with some reports that will save the accountant some time.

Once you've made your list, revise it. If someone else is interested in your business, ask for help. Try to think of every possible thing you can do with your computer, and don't overlook the "soft" uses, such as using your computer as a promotional aid. There are a lot of things that you don't do because you don't have time. Can any of these things be done by a computer?

The four remaining questions should be fairly easy once you've answered question one carefully. Information or data is of little use to you if you have to spend a great deal of time interpreting it. Do you need word descriptions of items or will numbers do? What form do you want this data in? What form do you have it in now and how can you improve it?

How much information will you need to store? Data storage capacity can be expensive. A moderate increase in your storage requirements can, in some cases, increase the cost of your system by as much as 50 percent or more. The little 5¼-inch diskette systems can store 160K or more on a single diskette. The 8-inch systems store more but cost a lot more, and the hard disk systems that store millions of items of data are big buck items.

Therefore, take care in answering question three. Break your needs down into two categories, short-term and long-term. Short-term should mean only data referred to and used daily. You'll be surprised at how little this really is. You should look at computers that can handle about double your short-term load. You don't want to run out of memory right in the middle of order processing, but you don't want to buy more than you need. As a general rule, one 8½ × 11-inch double spaced, typewritten page requires a little less than 2K of memory for storage. Many small business needs can be met with 48K and one or two 5¼-inch disk drives. The 48K will hold less than 24 pages of data, since you'll have to have some memory space for the computer program itself.

Question four is a matter of form. Just as you have some preferred ways of getting data out, you probably have a preferred method of putting it in. If you answered the first three

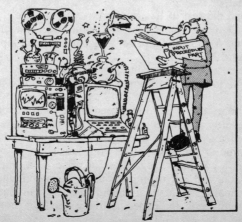

questions carefully, you know the answer to question four. One of the three primary resources is time. Don't waste time by using a computer that has a complicated input procedure.

A computer can help you get the most from your three resources but you have to determine how. This is the purpose of question five. Make three lists with these headings: time, talent, treasure. Under each item, jot down ways you can optimize how these resources are used. For instance, under "treasure," can you manage your cash better? You might list all of your clerical and managerial needs under "talent" and analyze each. Are you getting the most effective use out of your employees? Most managers are real experts at operating machines; can you say the same thing about the people who work for you?

WHERE TO GO FROM HERE

If it sounds like you need a computer to figure all of this out, then you've discovered at least one managerial use for a computer. But you need to analyze these things even if you don't have a computer. Here is a plan that will probably work for you:

1: Get out a pencil and paper. Take a pass at answering the five key questions and at answering the other questions posed in this chatper.

2. Read the rest of this book.

3. Read some other books and some magazine articles on the subject. You'll find a list of magazine and book publishers in Chapter 12.

4. Decide how much you can afford to spend.

5. Talk to several different vendors and look at lots of computers.

6. Before buying anything, read some more, if possible.

7. Develop an awareness of what will really be required to implement a system in your business. Be prepared to spend enough time to determine all of your needs.

Buying a computer, regardless of price, is a major undertaking. You will get the most out of your computer if you carefully analyze your situation and buy a system that fits both your current needs and expected future needs.

CHAPTER 8

The Stuff That Makes It Happen: Software

For the beginner, computers often appear just short of magical. Even with their covers off, computers give few hints of how they operate. There are no gears turning, no dials revealing telltale signs of activity.

The working components of small computers are integrated circuits (ICs) which have no moving parts. In fact, most of an IC is just protective plastic. Sealed inside all that plastic is a tiny silicon chip which does all the work. The silicon chip is so small it can be placed on the tip of your finger with room left for several thousand angels (at least) to dance around, too.

If computer machinery seems mysterious, computer software is equally amazing. If the computer were a kitchen (with the stove the CPU, or Central Processing Unit) the software would be a recipe to be followed. Just as there are many different types of recipes, so too are there many different types of software.

Some of the programs you will use were probably written in *machine language*, for example. Most software, however, is written in one of the *higher-level* languages.

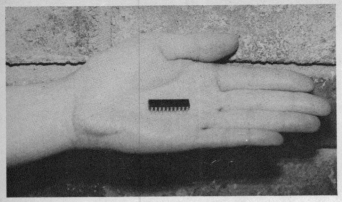

An integrated circuit

We don't want you to get the impression that you must learn to program a computer to be able to use it. It is nice to be able to write some of your own programs, or to at least know enough to modify and adapt the programs written by others. It really isn't necessary, though. (How many of us really know how our stereo works?) With the boom in small computers that has occurred over the last six years, there are thousands of programs just sitting on dealers' shelves or waiting in the computer magazines.

We have said it several times but it bears repeating: you don't have to master computer programming to use a small computer. There are plenty of canned programs out there that run on your computer. Just like recorded music, all you have to do is load the program into the computer's memory and run it. Jerry's 11-year-old daughter, Amy, uses her computer regularly with all sorts of educational programs and games. Although Amy uses her computer often, she has not yet mastered BASIC, the most common computer language today. All she has to do to run her favorite programs is insert a cartridge and tell the computer to load a program from the tape recorder. When the computer tells her it is ready, Amy can tell the computer to begin executing the instructions in the program. Perhaps later she will tackle BASIC or PILOT. For now, she's convinced computers are fun machines.

LANGUAGES FOR COMPUTERS

The computer in your home or business probably speaks several languages. No, it won't converse fluently in French or Spanish but it will probably speak BASIC, maybe Pascal or PILOT, and probably some dialect of a cryptic group of languages called machine language.

The particular CPU chip used in a computer determines which machine language it speaks. The Apple II computer, for example, has a 6502 CPU chip in it. Not unexpectedly, the Apple II speaks 6502 machine language. The TRS-80 from Radio Shack and the NorthStar Horizon computer both speak Z80 machine language since they have Z80 CPU chips.

Although much of the software in a computer is written in machine language, most beginners will want to leave that lan-

guage to the experienced programmer. It is hard to use, very tedious, and time-consuming for the programmer. To use it requires some dedicated study of the machine language used in your system. Machine languages also use funny number systems (hexidecimal, octal, or—heaven forbid—binary) instead of the familiar family favorite, decimal. Here is an excerpt from a machine language program:

Column	1	2	3
	004000	072	LDA
	004001	037	
	004002	006	
	004003	117	MOV C,A

All the numbers are written in octal, a base-8 number system. The first column of numbers (004000) specifies the memory cell in the computer where the instruction is to be placed. The second column (072) lists the actual instructions. Computers don't understand words or letters, so everything must be converted to numbers before the CPU chip can actually process the information. The 072 in the first line of this excerpt will cause the computer to perform a particular function. In this case it takes the two numbers that immediately follow the instruction (037 and 006 in this program) and puts them in a special storage location inside the CPU chip. The last column lists a shorthand summary of what the computer will do as the instructions are executed. The term LDA, for example, stands for Load the Accumulator with the contents of the memory location selected by the numbers that follow. MOV C,A means move whatever is in storage location A to storage location C. The computer only deals with the numbers in the second column, the machine language instructions. (The first column tells the programmer where to put the instructions in the computer's memory and the third column is helpful when you want to read the listing of a machine language program and figure out what's happening.)

It takes thousands of machine language instructions to perform even a simple job like keeping track of a list of names that will be printed on mailing labels. Again, we would suggest that you wade into machine language programming only after you've gained a lot of experience with an easier language like BASIC.

In between BASIC and machine language is something called *assembly language*. Remember LDA and MOV C,A in the previous excerpt? Using a special program called an *Assembler*, it is possible to type in phrases like LDA and MOV C,A and have them automatically converted into the proper machine language codes by the computer. Since it is much easier to remember what MOV C,A means than it is to remember numbers like 117, assembly language work is a lot easier than machine language. It is still necessary to know the intimate details of machine language programming, however, before assembly language work can be done. Take heart, though, there is another way.

Higher-level languages allow a beginner to start working with the computer in a very short period of time. This family of languages uses English-like words and mostly decimal numbers in the programming process. The best known of these languages, BASIC, is easy to learn. A weekend's work with a good BASIC book is enough to get a person started nicely. (There are over 100 BASIC books in print. For instance, di-lithium Press publishes an excellent book called *Instant Freeze Dried Computer Programming in BASIC*, *2nd Astounding Edition*, by Jerald R. Brown.) BASIC stands for Beginners All-Purpose Symbolic Instruction Code. Here is an example of a BASIC program:

```
10 PRINT "HELLO, WHAT IS YOUR NAME?"
20 INPUT N$
30 PRINT "WELL,",N$, "I'M GLAD YOU'VE COME
   OVER. I WAS LONELY."
```

As you can see, BASIC is more familiar than machine or assembly language. In BASIC each line of instructions has a line number. The three lines shown here are numbered in increments of 10. They could have been numbered 1, 2, and 3 or 49, 61, and 333. The computer doesn't care. It is best to always leave plenty of room between lines just in case you need to go back and add extra lines to the program. Between line 10 and line 20 in this program at least nine more lines could be added (e.g., 11, 12, 13, and so on). Some BASICs even allow line numbers such as 10.2 and 10.3.

BASIC understands a set of keywords which have a specific meaning for the computer. In the example the keywords PRINT and INPUT were used. Another keyword in BASIC is RUN. If you typed the three-line program into your computer and then typed RUN, the computer would begin executing the program. That is, it would look for the line with the smallest number (in this case line 10) and follow the instructions given there. Line 10 tells the computer to print the material between the quotation marks on the screen. Thus:

HELLO, WHAT IS YOUR NAME?

would appear on the screen. They keyword in line 20 is INPUT. It tells the computer to stop and wait for you to type in something on the keyboard. Suppose you type in CHARLIE. The computer takes CHARLIE and assigns it to the label N$. Now N$ equals CHARLIE. In line 30 the computer finds another PRINT instruction. It will print the following on the screen.

WELL, CHARLIE, I'M GLAD YOU CAME OVER.
I WAS LONELY.

The computer printed everything inside the quotation marks just as it appeared (e.g., "WELL" and "I'M GLAD YOU CAME OVER. I WAS LONELY.") The N$ is not enclosed in quotation marks, however. Instead of printing out N$, the computer looked at its list of labels and found that N$ stands for CHARLIE. Thus it printed CHARLIE instead of N$.

BASIC is, without question, the most popular small computer language today. It is used for a wide variety of applications from games to business to science and so on. More people work with BASIC than with FORTRAN or COBOL or any other language. There are, however, at least a hundred other high-level languages, each with a group of supporters who believe their language is the best. Some of the other languages are specialized. PILOT, for example, is designed expressly for educational applications.

Others are general-purpose languages which were written because someone saw deficiencies in the currently available languages. One of the general-purpose languages, Pascal, is currently developing a large following among small computer users. Some say it will replace BASIC in a few years as *the* language. Perhaps.

We do not want to leave you with the impression that BASIC is a single language and that BASIC on ATARI is the same as BASIC on a TRS-80 or an Apple II. BASIC is actually a family of languages. While it is relatively easy to shift from one version to another, there are real differences among the BASICs supplied with different small computers. Some of these differences reflect nothing more than the personality traits and preferences of the programmers who designed the BASICs. Other differences reflect the increased power and usefulness of some BASICs. The versions of BASIC for the ATARI computer or the Commodore Model 64 computer, for example, have some very powerful instructions for creating color graphics and for producing computer generated sounds and music. For example, if you want to draw a line on the screen, you can use the PLOT instruction to tell the computer where to start the line and use the DRAWTO instruction to tell it where the line should end.

TYPES OF COMPUTER SOFTWARE

Another difficult concept for novices has to do with the different types of software that run in computers. In this section we will deal with four types of software: languages, operating systems, utility software, and applications software.

Languages

Computer languages have already been discussed. Some computer manufacturers put the instructions that allow their system to "speak" BASIC, Pascal, and other high-level languages in ROM (Read Only Memory). If BASIC is in ROM the computer is usually ready to speak BASIC when it is switched on. Other manufacturers put BASIC and other languages on diskettes.

That means you must tell the computer to find the instructions on the diskette and load them into RAM (Random Access Memory) before the computer can speak BASIC.

Operating Systems

An operating system is a set of instructions, written in machine language, that lets you use all the pieces of your computer as an integrated computer system. Operating systems allow you, for example, to tell the computer to send information to the printer, the disk drive, or the video display. The operating system software for a computer is often in ROM and thus available for use as soon as the computer is switched on.

Operating systems that include instructions for disk drive operations are called *Disk Operating Systems* or *DOS*. A common pattern today is to put just enough of an operating system in ROM to allow the computer to load a larger DOS into RAM from a diskette.

Utility Programs

A type of program that does work very similar to that of operating systems is the utility program. A utility program is written to accomplish a specific, but routine job. There are several utility programs, for example, that allow you to use your small computer as a terminal which can communicate with larger computers over phone lines. Another type of utility program checks to see that the computer's memory, disk system, and video display are operating properly. Some diagnostic utility programs even tell you which chip needs to be replaced!

Applications Software

The final category of software to be discussed is the one we deal with most directly, applications programs. An applications program is a set of instructions that does something useful. Game programs, word processors, accounting software, electronic spreadsheet software, and educational programs are all *applications software*. Applications software can be written in a higher-level language like BASIC or in machine language. The distinguishing feature is not the language it is written in, but the fact that the software does something useful. Applications software can be purchased on cassette tapes, on diskettes, and in ROM chips that are installed in your computer.

There are tens of thousands of applications programs available today for small computers. They range in price from less than $10 for a simple game program to well over $10,000 for some special purpose programs (e.g., a program for grain elevator operators or a program that keeps track of pharmacy prescription records).

THE SPECIAL CASE OF CP/M

One of the problems faced by companies that write applications software for small computers is the issue of compatibility. A program written to operate on a NorthStar computer, for example, must be set up to operate under NorthStar DOS. Unfortunately, NorthStar Dos is not compatible with the DOS or disk operating systems of other computers such as Radio Shack, Apple, Cromemco, and so forth. That means a company writing applications programs must write a different version of each program for each brand of computer—a costly and time consuming task. Fortunately, there is another option if your computer has disk drives.

The most popular operating system is Digital Research's *CP/M* or *Control Program for Microcomputers*. It is not written for a particular computer. Instead, there are versions of CP/M for hundreds of different computers. CP/M is the closest thing we have today to a universal operating system for small computers. If you own a computer that can use CP/M you have a choice of buying applications software packages that run under the DOS designed specifically for your computer, or packages that run under CP/M.

Since it takes thousands of hours of effort to produce a major piece of applications software, many software companies prefer to write programs that run under CP/M. The same amount of effort produces a program that can be sold to owners of many different brands of computers. This is especially true of applications programs intended for the business/professional market. There are very few recreational programs for CP/M.

There are many different operating systems for computers today, and there are several that make an effort to be somewhat universal as does CP/M. For the moment, however, CP/M is the most widely accepted operating system. There is more good CP/M compatible business software available than any other type. It may be too much to hope for, but an equivalent of CP/M for computers used mainly for recreational or educational uses would enable the owner of one brand of computer to run software from many different suppliers. There are rumors of such things in the future, but for the present no such thing exists. Recreational and educational software can generally be used only on the specific computer for which it was written.

CHAPTER 9

It's Not Magic: The Basic Computer

When we first became interested in computers we read everything we could about the way computers work. We learned about computer memories, the signals that go out on parallel ports, handshaking, UARTS, RAM, ROM, integrated circuits, system clocks, data registers, and much more. The plain fact of the matter, however, is that you don't really have to know much about what goes on inside the computer to use it, just as you don't have to know a lot about a videotape machine or a microwave oven to use them.

It's nice to know how to build accessories for your own computer and how to troubleshoot problems when they occur. But gaining that much knowledge takes a great deal of time and effort—effort which might be better invested in something else, such as learning how to program the computer. Then you would be able to write or customize your own software. Our advice is to learn a little bit about hardware so you can carry on idle conversation at a party. Then concentrate on learning the software side of computing. Finally, after you've become proficient at programming in a computer language or two, go back to the hardware and dig a little deeper. For most people,

128

developing software skills pays off quicker. There is so much that can be done, and even a little knowledge of a popular language like BASIC can be of great benefit. Many people, in fact, will probably never get too involved with hardware. They will, instead, invest learning time in sharpening their software expertise. This makes a great deal of sense. Technological advances in computer hardware can make much of what you've learned obsolete in a very short time. This is less likely to happen to a person who has learned to program a computer. Programming or software knowledge is also more portable than hardware knowledge. If you learn to program your computer in BASIC, Pascal, or PILOT, it won't be too difficult to switch to an improved model or to a new system which also uses a similar language.

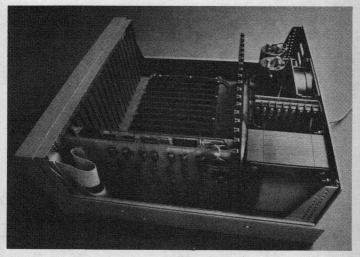

Interior of a small computer

The remainder of this chapter presents a brief overview of a typical computer system. If this introduction to hardware only whets your appetite, the dilithium Press catalog contains a number of books which concentrate on computer hardware.

A SIMPLE COMPUTER SYSTEM

Figure 9.1 shows a typical entry-level computer system. While the printer may be a bit of an extravagance for the beginner, it is an absolute necessity for anyone who plans to use the computer for word processing or business applications. Computer systems from several manufacturers include all of the components shown opposite, except the printer. In some cases the video monitor and the tape recorder are *optional* accessories. However, since you must have a monitor and a recorder to use the computer, they really aren't optional—they just cost extra. Let's take a look at each of the components that make up a typical small computer system.

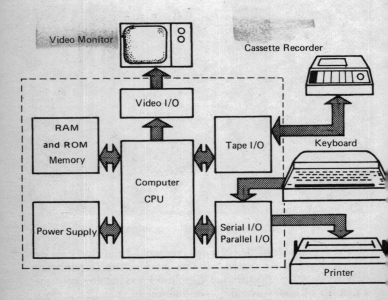

Figure 9.1 A typical small computer system

Power Supply

Not long ago power supplies for small computers were heavy brutes, designed to feed carefully filtered electrical energy to power-hungry circuits. Memory chips had particularly voracious appetites in the early microcomputers. Today, memory technology has progressed to the point where small computers require very little power. This has allowed designers to build smaller, less expensive power supplies which do a good job. The power supply alone in the old Sol 20 computer, for example, weighed twice as much as an Apple II computer and several VICs.

Most computer systems require at least two voltages, $+5$ and $+12$. Other commonly used voltages include -5 and -12 volts. The power supply takes 115 volts AC (alternating current) from your wall plug and converts to the DC (direct current) voltages required by the computer.

The power supply also does another job. It filters the line voltage so that a circuit that requires $+5$ volts gets just that, no more and no less. Power supplies which lack adequate

filtering tend to have *ripple* in their output. This means that the voltage sent to the computer will average +5 volts but many actually waver or ripple above and below 5 volts. Ripple can cause major problems in a computer. Fluctuations in the power supply voltage can cause the system to malfunction or behave in an erratic manner.

Most of the current crop of computers have adequate power supplies. Many of the small computers have a simple power supply designed to provide power only for the computer itself. Each additional accessory is supplied with its own power supply. This approach means you will have lots of power cords snaking around the computer if you add several accessories to your system. To make things a little neater we generally buy a powerstrip at a local hardware store or computer center and plug all our cords into the strip. Then we can turn the system on or off simply by throwing the switch on the power strip. Radio Shack, in fact, sells a power strip that has a built-in filter, a circuit breaker, an on-light, and a switch, all for about $50.

One more point should be made abour power supplies. A large number of problems associated with the use of small computers in homes and businesses are due to line voltage fluctuations. Suppose, for example, that you have a very large central air conditioning unit on the same circuit as your com-

A computer power supply

puter. The computer may work flawlessly in the winter and work poorly or not at all in the summer. Line voltage may drop considerably when a heavy demand is placed on the line. This phenomenon has become commonplace in many parts of the country and is known as *brownout*. Few computer power supplies are designed to deal with extreme fluctuations in line voltages. There are, however, a number of companies that sell special transformers which maintain a constant output voltage over a wide range of input voltages. Though expensive, in some environments they may be the only way to obtain dependable operation from a computer.

Radio Shack surge protector

A related problem that can drive a computer user up the wall is a power line *glitch*. A glitch is a very brief spike of high voltage. Although the typical wall plug will provide around 115 volts, there are circumstances which may, for a fraction of a second, produce several thousand volts on the line. The erratic operation of one of our computers was finally traced to a large motor which was used to move air in a chilled water air conditioning system. Each time the motor turned on it caused the line voltage to drop slightly. It turned out that the power supply in our computer could handle that. When the motor turned off, however, it created a collapsing electrical field which fed a high voltage spike, or glitch, back into the electrical wiring of the building. Since it lasted only a split second, the most anyone ever noticed was a bit of static on the radio. But even that brief instant of high voltage was anathema to the computer. The spike rode into the power supply on the power line and was fed into the computer where it managed to royally confuse things. Programs that were working perfectly suddenly ran amuck. An automotive parts supply company which was on the same power line as a welding shop experienced similar problems whenever the electrical welders were in use. Again, most computer power supplies were not designed to handle such a problem, but there are several brands of power line isolators and filters on the market. They typically cost $40 to $80 and can often cure glitchitis immediately.

Memory

Computers need quite a bit of memory or storage capability. All the instructions a computer follows, for example, must be stored somewhere in memory. Data to be analyzed is also usually stored in the computer's memory.

A computer's memory works much like a human memory. Information to be used later is stored as electrical charges in memory *cells*. These are actually tiny sections on a wafer of silicon that can be charged by an electrical impulse. The memory of most computers is organized into *eight-bit bytes*. A bit is simply a place where a single piece of data is stored. A computer can store one *bit* in each memory cell. A bit can be either a 1 (on) or a 0 (off). Generally, a cell that has an electrical charge in it is considered to be holding a 1, while a cell with no charge in it is a 0.

By themselves, the lowly bits can't do much. To make them more useful they are combined into *bytes*. This is a bit, 0, and this is a byte: 00110011. A byte is simply a set of eight bits. There are only two possible patterns for a bit, 1 and 0, but there are 256 possible patterns for a byte. Computers have been programmed to treat each byte pattern as a code which can stand for a letter, number, or instruction. Computers can't deal directly with the letter A, but they can deal with a byte (a pattern of eight bits) which stands for A. The most commonly used code today is ASCII or American Standard Code for Information Interchange. The ASCII code for A is 01000001. Upper-and lower-case letters, the numbers from 0 to 9, the most commonly used punctuation marks, and numerous computer control codes each have their own unique eight-bit code in ASCII. Since the computer must deal with eight-bit bytes of data, the computer's memory is also organized into eight-bit bytes. If someone says their computer has 8K of memory, that translates into 8192 bytes of memory. The term K is an abbreviation for 1024. Thus 8K equals 8×1024 or 8192. Each byte of memory can hold the code for one letter or number. Since a typical, double-spaced, typewritten page will have less than 2000 characters on it, 8K of memory will hold about four full pages. That really isn't much, which explains why most computers used for word processing have at least 32K of memory, enough to hold over 16 pages.

As Figure 9.1 shows, there are two major types of memory, *ROM* and *RAM*. ROM stands for *Read Only Memory*. This kind of memory is generally programmed at the factory. The contents of ROM cannot be changed by the user. The Radio

Shack computers, for example, store the instructions for their version of BASIC in ROM. Other computer manufacturers sell much of their software in ROM. The game cartridges you buy for those video game machines, in fact, are nothing more than several ROM chips encased in a protective plastic package. In computers like the Exidy Sorcerer, the Commodore VIC, the ATARI computers, and the Radio Shack Color Computer, ROMs containing instructions for programs can be inserted into slots in the side or top of the computer.

A Sorcerer "ROMPAC"

To clarify the point, we should note that if we took off the case of the ROM cartridges we would find a small circuit board with several integrated circuits on it. Most of the integrated circuits (ICs for short) would be ROM chips. By packaging most of the ROMs for their computer in removable cartridges, several manufacturers have made it easier to use the computer for many different jobs. Some computer manufacturers, for example, put the ROM that contains BASIC on the main computer board. It cannot be removed and thus takes up room in the computer's *memory map* whether it is being used or not. Most of the small computers priced at under $1000 can only accept a little over 64,000 bytes of memory. If a ROM with BASIC in it takes up 16,000 bytes of memory space all the time, that means there is only 48K of memory space available for other uses. Unless a computer is to be used for only one purpose, it is better to have as much of the ROM as possible in removable cartridges rather than installed permanently. If the ROMs containing BASIC can be removed you will be able to use the same memory space for another ROM cartridge containing a language such as PILOT.

All computer memory cannot be ROM, however. Much of the memory in a computer is *Random Access Memory* or *RAM*. The average home computer will contain 16K of RAM, while a business computer system often has 64K or more of RAM, in addition to some ROM. Newer systems may have over 500K of RAM. RAM is also known as *volatile* memory and is general-purpose memory. You can store data or instructions in RAM, then tell the computer to use the information you've stored in RAM, and then replace the material in RAM with something new. The biggest problem with RAM is that whatever is in it disappears when the computer is turned off. If you need to save something in RAM for use later, you must store it on tape or on disk before the computer is shut down. (Material in ROM remains there essentially forever.)

A computer memory board

Suppose you are using your computer as a word processor to write a paper or report. As you type in new material it appears on the screen. It is also stored in RAM memory. As you edit the document, the material in RAM changes to reflect your modifications. Suppose now that it is late at night and you decide to stop and get some sleep. You will finish the paper in the morning. You could leave the computer on all night, but if the power went off even for a split second everything in RAM would be lost. All you need to do to avoid that very unpleasant possibility is to tell the computer to save your work on a diskette. You might use an instruction like this: SAVE "MYPAPER" which means the material in RAM which you just typed in will be saved or stored on a diskette under the name MYPAPER. Now with a copy of the material on the diskette, you can switch the computer off and sleep peacefully. The next morning it is only necessary to insert the diskette into the disk drive and tell the computer to load the material named MYPAPER back into RAM.

I/O Ports — A port is a sort of gate or entryway into the computer. Data flows into and out of the computer through a variety of *I/O* or *Input/Output ports*. These ports generally consist of some electronic circuits and a plug or connection that mates the computer with another device such as a printer or a television screen.

Video Display Ports — It requires quite a bit of hardware and software to display the data stored in a computer's memory in orderly rows on a video screen. Most computers will display at least 24 lines of 40 characters or 16 lines of 64 characters on a television screen or video monitor. Most also permit you to display a variety of graphic figures and symbols. Graphic figures can be combined to create pictures, charts, and illustrations. Some computers have special circuits that give them very sophisticated graphics features.

Cassette I/O — The least expensive method of storing computer data is on a good tape recorder. All the major small computers currently available have built-in cassette I/O features. The cassette system converts all the little ASCII bits and bytes into tones which are stored on tape. To put this taped data back into the computer's memory you reverse the process. The tones on the tape are converted back into 1s and 0s, collected into bytes, and stored in RAM.

Disk I/O — This is really a special version of a *serial* or *parallel* I/O which will be discussed later, but it is important enough to be treated separately here. Cassette storage systems are slow and sometimes unreliable. Disk storage is fast and very reliable. In some computers, the circuits required to send data to and from disk drives are inside the computer. The Radio Shack Model IV, for example, has a disk controller board inside the computer enclosure. Other computers use smart disk drives which contain their own controller circuits. The ATARI computers and the Commodore computers both use *smart* disk systems. The 8050 disk drive from Commodore holds half a million bytes of data on each diskette! Smart disk systems generally cost more, but can be installed by the owner in a minute or two.

A floppy diskette looks a lot like a thin 45 RPM record enclosed in a protective envelope. The *platter* inside the envelope is made of mylar and covered with a magnetic coating that can be magnetized by a recording head inside the disk drive. As the drive spins the floppy disk, the head presses against the platter and reads the information stored on it or writes new information on it. Most computers allow you to connect at least four disk drives. The number of drives, however, is not the most important number. The 810 disk drive from Atari can store 80K of data on a diskette while the Commodore 8050 can store 500K, the equivalent of six ATARI drives. The 8050, as you might expect, is more expensive than the ATARI drive, but it is not six times as expensive.

Serial and Parallel I/O — There are two types of general purpose I/O ports in small computers. These ports are called *parallel* and *serial*. A parallel port has a wire or connection for each of the eight bits in a byte of data. If you tell the computer to send a byte out a parallel port to a printer, all eight bits in the byte are shipped out to the printer at the same time over eight different lines. Generally, input from the keyboard to the computer is also through a parallel port. The term *Centronics compatible port* refers to a relatively standard parallel port to which a printer can be attached. (Centronics is a printer manufacturer.) If your printer also has a parallel interface, you will probably be able to connect it to a Centronics compatible I/O port on the computer.

Serial I/O ports work a bit differently from parallel ports. When eight bits of data arrive at a serial port, they don't all leave at the same time. Instead, the first bit in a byte is sent out on one line, then the next bit goes out on the same line, and so on. All the bits in each byte march out of the computer (or into the computer) over the same line. Any work that involves transmitting data over telephone lines will use a serial port.

The term *baud rate* is often used in relation to serial ports. Telephone couplers (modems) generably work at a speed of *300 baud*. Simply defined, a baud rate of 300 is equivalent to a speed of around 350 words per minute. Last year we bought a small printer that could be connected to a serial I/O port. Since our computers all had serial I/O ports we assumed it would plug right in. Unfortunately, the fine print in the printer manual told us it accepted data only at a speed of 600 baud while our computers transmitted at only 300 or 1200 baud. Read the fine print as well as the bold before buying.

You will often see the term *RS-232* or *RS-232C* in advertisements for computers and computer peripherals. The RS-232 standard (the C is often left off) is a set of defined characteristics for a serial I/O port. If you have a printer with a serial interface, or a telephone coupler (modem) that is RS-232 compatible, you should be able to plug them into your serial port on the computer. However, since printer and modem manufacturers wire their RS-232 connections slightly differently (the proper signals are on different pins), it may be necessary to get someone at the local computer store to wire up a cable for you.

Game Paddle, Joystick, and Light Pen I/O Ports — These are all special versions of a parallel (sometimes serial) I/O port designed specifically for a particular device. Computers that have such ports are more versatile.

CPU

The *CPU*, or *central processing unit*, is the heart of a computer system. Although most CPU chips are smaller than an Oreo cookie, the electronic components they contain would have filled a room a few decades ago. Using advanced microelectronic techniques, manufacturers can cram thousands of circuits into tiny silicon chips that work dependably and use less power than an electric razor. There are several manufacturers of CPU chips. Intel makes the 8080, the 8085, 8086, 8088, and several others. Zilog makes the Z80 and the Z-8000; Motorola makes the 6800 and the 68000; and Commodore makes the 6502 used in Apple II, ATARI, and PET computers. While there are real differences among the CPU chips men-

A CPU chip

tioned above, the differences are mainly of interest to computer designers and experienced programmers. You can work with your computer a long time without even knowing which chip it uses. (Do you know what type of engine you have in your car?) You don't need to know anything about the internal workings of your computer.

Regardless of the chip, the CPU does all the actual processing inside the computer. It also sends signals to the other parts of the computer which synchronize the operation of each component. This synchronization permits the system to perform thousands of operations a second. These operations are fairly simple (e.g., adding two numbers together) but the speed at which they are done allows the computer to do some very complex things by breaking complicated jobs into hundreds of simple steps.

CHAPTER 10

The Current Crop

We subscribe to over 40 computer periodicals and attend our share of conventions, conferences, and trade shows each year. A rough guess would be that through these various outlets computer manufacturers announce ten new systems a month. The companies that offer these new machines to the public range in size from billion dollar multinationals to one-person operations occupying half of a two-car garage. The products offered enter a marketplace where a large assortment of computers are already competing hotly for the consumer's dollar. The abundance of computer models makes choosing a computer difficult, but it also means that you can probably buy a computer system that fits your needs.

Since the publication of the first edition of this book (1981) many new models have appeared. Surprisingly, however, few of the computers reviewed in the first edition have been discontinued. This chapter reviews 44 different models; the first edition reviewed less than twenty.

We have divided this chapter into three sections. The first section covers *Current Popular Computers* in some detail. The next section, *New Models and Some Sleepers*, reviews some of the models which were just beginning to show up in the stores as this chapter was written. We have also included a few computers which have been on the market for some time but which are not among the most successful systems of their type. Finally, there is a section that deals briefly with *Other Computers of Interest*. The computers in this section may be older models with a small group of devoted users, new models which do not have strong dealer networks, or simply computers for which we could find very little information. Also included here are some of the high quality business computers that generally are not purchased for personal use, but which do well in the business market.

Before we can discuss the currently available computers, we need to define some terms and outline the pattern of our reviews:

Video Display — This is the screen on the computer. If a display is 16 by 32, it is 16 lines long and 32 characters wide. Remember that spaces, periods, commas, etc., are all counted as characters. Video displays may be color or black and white.

Keyboard — The keyboard is often described as a standard, full-size unit. Standard keyboards have a QWERTY layout. This means that they are about the size of a standard typewriter keyboard and the key arrangement is the same. QWERTY refers to the layout of the third row of keys—QWERTYUIOP.

A keyboard may also have a separate numeric keypad. This is a separate set of keys laid out in standard calculator fashion. The keypad may be an important feature if you plan to use the computer for business or educational applications.

Some keyboards have keys for letters, numbers, punctuation symbols and little else. Other keyboards have *function* keys that allow you to give the computer some instructions by pressing one function key. A few systems even have programmable function keys so that you can program a key to issue an instruction or command you use often.

RAM — Computers vary in the amount of memory available to the user.

Languages Used — These are the programming languages available for use on the computer. Examples include BASIC, Pascal, assembler, FORTRAN, PILOT, and Logo. If you plan to write your own programs you will want to pick a computer with a language you can use.

Storage — These are the methods available for storing your programs. Most computers have a cassette tape interface or a floppy disk interface. Many have both, although the disk interface is usually an extra cost option.

Software — We will give you an idea of the type of applications programs available for each computer. If you don't plan to write your own programs, you will want a system with lots of software available from the manufacturer and from independent software developers.

I/O Ports — These are the number and type of input/output ports available for connecting the computer to various peripherals. If you plan to buy a large system, a computer equipped with several serial and parallel I/O ports can save you money in the long run since there will be fewer options to buy.

Service — This refers to the likelihood of repairs and the prospects of getting your computer repaired when necessary. Our information on new models will, of course, be limited since it is difficult to guess how well all the promises of great service and support will be kept.

Price — We generally will not list the price of a system unless it is unusual (e.g., the Commodore VIC is very inexpensive; the Grid Compass is very expensive). There are several reasons for not including prices in this section. First, there is generally not a *set* price for a particular model. Dealers in competitive markets generally offer discounts of 5 percent to 10 percent. Second, the pricing of computers is not always a rational process in which a manufacturer totals up the cost of

producing and distributing his product, adds in a decent profit, and then sets the retail price. The price tag on many models is determined by the price of competing units. It is not unusual for the price of a particular computer to change by several hundred dollars over a short period of time as new competition dictates adjustments.

The job of selecting a computer is the topic of other chapters. Since we can't possibly cover all of the several hundred models, we concentrate on describing the most popular computers on the market today. The computers we chose are those that cost between $40 and $4000 dollars. They represent over 95 percent of the small computer market. We will start with the machines from the company that has more retail outlets for their computers than anyone else, Tandy Corporation.

Current Popular Computers

THE RADIO SHACK COMPUTERS

There are currently six different Radio Shack computers. Radio Shack sells its computers through company-owned Radio Shack stores and computer centers, and through franchised dealers who carry Radio Shack products in their own stores. In addition, Radio Shack computers, particularly the TRS-80 Model 4, are sold by hundreds of mail order discount houses who buy the basic computer, add their own accessories and sell them at lower prices than Radio Shack itself.

TRS-80 Model 4

This is an improved version of the very popular Model III computer. It is appropriate for home, educational, and business applications.

Video Display. The Model 4 has two operating modes. The *Model III mode* runs all the software written for the Model III computer. In this mode the video display puts 16 lines of 64 characters on the screen. Crude graphics are built in. There is also a 16 by 32 format that uses larger letters. Upper and lower case letters are standard. The built-in display has both contrast and brightness control. The built-in monitor is of good quality.

In the *Model 4 mode* the computer can handle 24 lines of 80 characters. The increased display capacity is only available, however, if you have software written specifically for the Model 4. Model III software uses the 16 by 64 format.

Keyboard. The keyboard on the Model 4 is a full-size, standard typewriter-style unit. It works well, but it has only a few function keys: four are user-programmable. A numeric keypad is standard.

RAM. The computer comes with 64K of RAM and can be expanded to 128K. If you buy a cassette version of the computer, you will not be able to take advantage of the extra memory. A cassette Model 4 is really a Model III computer which will not have desirable features such as an 80 column by 24 line display (the III has 16 lines of 64 characters). We therefore recommend you consider purchasing the Model 4 with disk drives.

Languages Used. BASIC is standard on the Model 4. The most widely used small computer BASIC, Microsoft BASIC, is available when the computer is turned on. In addition, virtually every general purpose computer language has been adapted for use on the Model 4. A number of companies other than Radio Shack market languages and disk operating systems for the computer. LDOS from Logical Systems is one of the better disk operating systems for the Model III computer. It appears that Radio Shack's disk operating system for the Model 4 is actually an enhanced LDOS. You thus get the power of a premium disk operating system on the Model 4 since LDOS is now the standard rather than an optional operating system.

Storage. You can use a standard cassette recorder to store programs and data on all versions of the Model 4. A cassette Model 4 is really a Model III computer with an improved keyboard. Disk drives (5 ¼-inch) are optional. Standard disks are single-sided, double density, and store about 170K. Radio Shack, as well as several other suppliers, have hard disk systems that plug into the Model 4.

Software. No other computer, with the possible exception of the Apple II, has more software written for it. The variety of software available from both Radio Shack and other vendors is one of the strongest selling points. Radio Shack has announced that an optional disk operating system called CP/M will be available for the Model 4. The ability to run CP/M on the Model 4 means that you will have access to several thousand programs. Most of the good business and managerial programs will run under CP/M.

I/O Ports. There is one built-in parallel port and one serial port in the disk version of the Model 4. Most of the software written for the computer assumes you will be using a parallel printer interface. If you use a serial printer interface, it generally will be necessary to tell the disk operating system that a serial rather than a parallel interface is in use.

Service. Radio Shack has a large number of regional repair centers; their computer centers also provide service. Our experience with Radio Shack service has been very disappointing, although this may not be representative. The cost of service was reasonable, but the quality was poor. Machines were returned without being repaired, and in some instances major repairs were performed (and paid for) that were not necessary. For example, one computer center replaced an entire disk drive for us. We later discovered that the only thing wrong with the system was that the cable had oxidized and worked loose from its connector. We recommend you purchase a service contract on your computer if you plan to use your computer heavily. We send most of our Radio Shack equipment that needs repair to a franchised dealer (Sounds, Etc., Watonga, OK) rather than to a company store. In your part of the country, however, it may be better to send your computer to a Radio Shack store since dealers and stores vary considerably.

TRS-80 Model 12

Video Display. The Model 12 comes with a built-in 12-inch, black and white video monitor that is very good. It displays 24 lines of 80 characters, upper and lower case. A format of 24 lines by 40 large characters can also be used. There are no standard graphics features, but an optional graphics board is available.

Keyboard. This business-oriented computer has an excellent typewriter-style keyboard with a number of extra function keys that make it very convenient to use. A numeric keypad is standard.

RAM. 80K is provided in a minimum system; 768K of memory is available. You must load the language to be used from diskette into memory.

Languages Used. The Model 12 comes with a sophisticated BASIC that uses 8-inch floppy diskettes for data and program storage. FORTRAN, COBOL, Pascal and virtually every other major computer language are available. All of these languages are on disk.

Storage. There is one 8-inch disk drive housed beside the monitor in the main computer cabinet. Three more can be added. Each disk can store about 1.25 million bytes of data. A hard disk system that stores 8.4 million bytes is also available. You can add up to four hard disks to a Model 12 system.

TRS-80 Model 12

Software. There is a large amount of high quality business and professional software available. Games are also available, but it would be hard to justify buying a $3200 computer just to play games. Many small businesses are buying this computer because it is reliable, it uses high capacity 8-inch disk drives, and there is lots of business software written for it.

I/O Ports. One parallel and two serial ports are standard. It is relatively easy to connect printers and modems. In addition, Radio Shack supplies several types of software that help the computer talk to printers, modems, and mainframe computers.

The Model 12 was designed for computing jobs that need more computing power than a Model IV has, but jobs that aren't big enough to justify an expensive minicomputer or mainframe. It is a relatively reliable system that does the work of a business or professional computer quite nicely. A particularly strong point for this computer is the number of independent companies writing software for it. You are not tied to one supplier for software, and you can buy accessories and peripherals from many sources as well.

TRS-80 Model 16

Viedo Display. A built-in 12-inch green video display uses a 24 by 80 format. Very good quality.

Keyboard. Same as the Modell II.

TRS-80 Model 16

RAM. 128K of RAM is standard; the computer can be expanded to 512K.

Languages/Software. This is a new model that has two microprocessor chips, the Z80A and the MC68000. The MC68000 is a new 16 *bit* chip manufactured by Motorola that can process data much faster than the 8 bit chips normally used in small computers. However, there is very little software currently available for the MC68000. When the Model 16 runs under the control of the Z80A chip from Zilog, it can run any of the software available for the Model 12. It remains to be seen just how well Radio Shack will support this new computer. Buyers who are not aware of the paucity of software are likely to be unhappy until software support improves.

Storage. The Model 16 comes with one double-sided, double density 8-inch disk drive built into the side of the monitor. One more can be added. Each diskette can store 1.2 million bytes of data. Up to four hard disk units can be connected, each capable of storing 8.4 million bytes of data.

I/O Ports. Like the Model II, there are two serial ports and one parallel port. In addition, the Model 16 is a *multi-user* computer. You can add two terminals to the system (around $650 each) so that up to three different users can work on the computer at the same time.

The Model 16 is Radio Shack's newest computer; it has received a good deal of attention in the computer press. It incorporates advanced technologies and has a huge memory and storage capacity compared to most other small computers. Its price tag of $5000 + reflects its extra features. The multi-user capacity, however, more than offsets the price *if* you need more than one user station and *if* Radio Shack is forthcoming with software that takes advantage of its advanced features. Some feel Radio Shack might have fared better if they had waited until they had more software available before putting the Model 16 on the market.

TRS-80 Color Computer

Video Display. The color display shows 26 lines of 32 characters in capital letters only. Limited color graphics are possible with the standrad BASIC supplied with the computer; more sophisticated color graphics features come with the extra-cost BASIC. This $299 computer attaches to your standard color television and uses either channel 3 or 4 for its display. Sharpness and clarity are good but not outstanding.

Keyboard. The system uses a standard typewriter format, but the keyboard is slightly smaller than a typewriter keyboard. If you are a touch typist the keys may feel a little strange. There are few function keys and no numeric keypad.

RAM. 4K of RAM is standard. You can add up to 32K of memory.

Language Used. There are two versions of BASIC for the Color Computer. Both are contained in ROM chips that plug into sockets inside the computer. The computer speaks BASIC when it's switched on. If you plan to use the color graphics features, buy the more expensive BASIC. Logo is also available for this computer; this is a strong selling point if you are shopping for a computer that young children are going to use.

Storage. Cassette storage is standard (but the cassette recorder itself is optional). You can also add 5¼-inch disk drives to the Color Computer. They store approximately 150K on each diskette.

Software. Radio Shack was a bit slow in producing software for this computer. Currently there are several games in ROM cartridges that plug into the side of the computer. There are also some programs on cassette tape. Other companies market software for the Color Computer, but there is less software available for it than for other computers with similar features.

TRS-80 Color Computer

I/O Ports. A serial port is standard. There are two *joystick* connectors which are used in many games. There is also a way of generating tones through the television speaker—another nice feature for games.

The Color Computer is an attractive system that is found mainly in homes. If there were more programs available, it would be more competitive with systems such as the ATARI 400 and the Commodore VIC.

TRS-80 Micro Color Computer

This machine was announced as this section was written. Therefore, information provided here is tentative. Radio Shack's Color Computer, described above, has run a distant fourth in the under-$300 computer market. The Timex Sinclair 1000, the Commodore VIC, and the ATARI 400 all had stronger sales than the Color Computer. The Micro Color Computer, priced at $120, appears to be Radio Shack's response to the Timex Sinclair, which has sales in the million-plus range.

Video Display. The Micro Color Computer (MC 10) attaches to your color or black and white television and displays 16 lines of 32 characters, upper case only. The computer has some graphics capability and can display in several colors. Sound synthesis is also possible.

Keyboard. The keyboard on this computer is laid out in the same way as a typewriter keyboard, but it is much smaller and the keys are of the square *chiclet* variety.

RAM. 4K of RAM is standard; up to 20K can be added by attaching memory cartridges to the back of the computer.

Languages Used. The BASIC built into this machine is similar to the BASIC on the Color Computer. Other languages are likely to be available for the MC-10, but none were available when this was written.

Software. Radio Shack plans to offer a range of software, particularly games and educational programs, for this computer. Little is available currently. Surprisingly, there is no ROM cartridge slot on the computer; you will have to load programs in from a cassette recorder (optional). In addition, the computer does not appear to be compatible with any other computer. Had it been software-compatible with the Color Computer, it would have been able to take advantage of the growing base of software for that machine. As it is, software availability is likely to be a major problem.

I/O Ports. Provisions for connecting a cassette recorder and a serial printer or modem are built in.

This computer is a bit puzzling. It is not an outstanding computer when compared to other machines in its price range and it has very little software available, while the lower priced Commodore VIC has plenty. This may be an example of too little and too late for Radio Shack.

Model 100

This is one of Radio Shack's newest models and one that represents a radically different approach to small computers. Made in Japan by the same company that produces the NEC portable computer, the Model 100 has many innovative features. It is battery operated, has a full-size keyboard, and uses a liquid crystal display with 8 lines of 40 characters. The computer comes standard with 8K of RAM and can accept as much as 32K of RAM.

The Model 100 is not a general purpose computer. Instead, it fills a market need between the handheld computers such as the Radio Shack PC-1 and the transportable computers such as the Osborne I. Handheld computers have limited features, and transportable models must be plugged into a power source to operate. The Model 100 runs on batteries that fit inside the case. Its keyboard is as good as many on regular personal computers, and the 8 by 40 display is sufficient for many uses. The $795 price for the basic computer includes some items that are normally options. There is a built-in modem, for example, that lets you connect the computer directly to the telephone line. A serial port is also provided along with a parallel printer port and a cassette interface port.

Standard software in ROM is also an impressive feature. The computer naturally speaks BASIC, but there is also a word processor, a scheduling program, telecommunications software, and an address file. It is also possible to use this computer while you are on the go and then transfer data from it to the Model IV when you return to your home base. That feature is likely to make this computer a popular accessory for Model IV owners.

The Radio Shack/Sharp Hand-Held Computers

Radio Shack's three hand-held or *pocket* computers are truly unique. They look like overgrown calculators, but they are much more than that. All three can be programmed in BASIC. They have calculator-style keyboards that include all the letters of the alphabet arranged just like a typewriter keyboard (a very small typewriter keyboard). A numeric keypad lies to the right of the letter keys. People with fat fingers will have trouble with this keyboard. There is a small liquid crystal display which has room for one line of 24 characters on the PC-1 and slightly more on the PC-2. Some limited graphics are possible on the PC-2 display. The PC-4 displays one line of 12 characters.

Smallness is the main feature of these computers. They fit in your pocket and run for 75 (PC-2) to 300 (PC-1) hours on

Radio Shack Pocket Computer

small batteries that fit inside the case. The RAM memory (1.9K in the PC-1, up to 4K in the PC-2) is kept on standby when the computer is turned off. That means a program you put into memory is not lost when the machine is switched off. The PC-1 sells for around $150, the PC-2 for $280, and the PC-4 for $70. Both can be used with a cassette tape recorder for data storage. The PC-1 and PC-4 have an optional printer that prints on a tiny roll of paper. The PC-2 has an amazing little built-in printer that prints characters and graphics in four colors.

If you are one of those people who need a small, portable, programmable computer, then you should give these computers serious consideration. A pilot, a construction engineer, and a real estate salesperson all come to mind; Radio Shack has inexpensive software packages for each. There are software packages for surveying, civil engineering, aviation, engineering math, real estate, business finance and statistics, and horse race analysis. Several games are also available.

Radio Shack's pocket computers are actually manufactured by Sharp Electronics in Japan. You can buy them from Radio Shack or from Sharp dealers.

APPLE COMPUTERS

Like Radio Shack, Apple must be considered one of the surviving *old line* companies in this business. Surviving, however, hardly describes the behavior of the Apple Computer Company. It is one of the dominant manufacturers in the field. Many predicted Apple would begin to falter as competition increased from Japanese manufacturers and from companies like IBM and Xerox. It hasn't faltered yet.

The Apple II computer is so popular that several companies now market *work-alike* computers that can run all the software that runs on the Apple II. The Franklin Ace 1000 is the best known of the Apple work-alikes.

Apple II

Video Display. The display shows 24 lines of 40 characters. Several levels of color graphics can be used, with quality ranging from crude to very good. The Apple II uses your color television (requires an extra-cost modulator) or a color monitor as its display. Several suppliers offer optional circuits that permit the Apple II to display upper and lower case letters and/or 80-character lines.

Keyboard. The system uses a standard typewriter-style keyboard of reasonable quality. Several third party suppliers sell higher quality keyboards that can replace the one that comes with the Apple II.

RAM. 64K is the minimum, but expansion to 124K is possible.

Languages Used. Apple offers several versions of BASIC in ROM, and other languages such as Pascal, PILOT, and Logo. You can also purchase a curcuit card that allows the Apple II to run the CP/M operating system and Z80-based software.

Storage. The standard Apple II uses regular cassettes for storage. Some people have complained about the reliability of the cassette storage system. Five-and-one-fourth-inch disk drives are also available. Other companies, including Corvus, offer hard disks for the Apple II.

Apple II

Software. The Apple II is one of the best-selling computers today. Its popularity has prompted many programmers to write or adapt software for it. There are thousands of business, home, recreational, and educational programs for the Apple II. Bell and Howell sells a modified Apple to the school market. Because it can display color graphics, the Apple II is used extensively in educational settings.

I/O Ports. Four game paddle ports are standard; two paddles are provided. The computer can create simple sounds through a speaker in the computer. Optional cards plug into slots in the computer to provide ports for printers, modems, and disk drives. Several companies, in addition to Apple Computer itself, specialize in building accessories for the Apple II. There is a great deal of sophisticated equipment for this computer including music synthesizers, home environmental and security controllers, laboratory data analyzers, and much more.

Service. Apple originally had some difficulty in this area. They now have a satisfactory system of regional and local repair depots, and a number of their dealers have very good repair facilities.

The Apple II has been a very successful computer. It brought the Apple Computer Company from facilities in part of a rented garage to the status of a multimillion dollar corporation whose stock sells on a major exchange. The system is best suited for educational and home applications. Business applications are possible but they may require quite a bit of additional equipment. Reasonable documentation, strong factory support and an enormous software base are all Apple strong points. The price of the Apple II (over $1500) is much higher than several other computers with equal or better hardware features. Many people still buy the Apple II, however, because owning the computer gives you access to an enormous variety of software. There are probably more books, accessories, and programming aids available for the Apple II than for any other computer.

Apple III

Video Display. The Apple III displays 24 lines of 80 characters, upper and lower case, in black and white. A black and white monitor is provided. The system will also support 40-character lines in color, but you must supply the color monitor or television. Color graphics like those on the Apple II are also possible. In addition, you can program the Apple III to display different character sets including non-English alphabets.

Keyboard. The high-quality standard keyboard includes a numeric keypad. A word processing version of the Apple III has control and editing functions printed on the keys, making them easier to use. The functions of the 74 keys on the keyboard can also be changed in software, making specialized programming applications much easier. It is one of the better small-computer keyboards.

RAM. 128K is standard. A full blown system can use a maximum of 256K.

Storage. The computer comes with one 5¼-inch disk drive built into the case. Three more can be added. Hard disk drives are also available.

Languages Used. Apple offers several versions of BASIC, including a high-powered business BASIC. Other languages such as Pascal are available, in addition to machine and assembly language. To some extent, these languages can be used cooperatively on the Apple III (e.g., create a file in one language, process it in another).

Software. The Apple III will run software written for the

Apple II, which means a great deal of software already exists for it. The new software designed specifically for the Apple III is primarily business and professional software. The Apple III has not been as popular as Apple hoped, and there is less independently produced software for it than for several other business-oriented systems in the same price range.

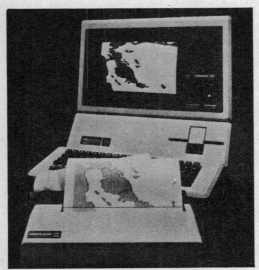

Apple III

I/O Ports. The Apple III uses the same format as the Apple II. Equipment that attaches to the Apple II should easily connect to the Apple III using the same interface cards. Two serial ports are included in the base price. In addition, there is a sound synthesizer which can be programmed to generate music and voicelike sounds.

This little computer has a base price of $3400, and by the time you add a printer and software it can easily take over $8000 to set up a complete system. It is designed for a segment of the small business and professional market which lies above the upper limits of the Apple II. The Apple III has been on the market for several years now, but design errors and production problems marred its first year. Sales were dismal. Apple now feels it has eliminated all the bugs, and released it again in 1981 as the "new, more powerful Apple III." By the time most of the problems were corrected, however, several other manufacturers had their small business models on the market. You should do quite a bit of comparison shopping before selecting the Apple III.

THE COMMODORE COMPUTERS

Commodore Business Machines was one of the first companies to market an appliance computer, a computer that could be taken home, plugged in, and used immediately. The early PET computers spoke BASIC when they were turned on, and they had built-in video displays and cassette recorders. The PET had built-in components before most of its competition.

Considering the head start that Commodore had, it is surprising to find that Commodore machines are only the fourth, fifth, or sixth most popular computers, depending on which statistics you believe. Why aren't they first or second? There were technical problems with some of the first models. Commodore was unresponsive to owners who needed help; it treated their dealers in ways that made them look for other brands to carry; and it discouraged third party software.

While Commodore's market share suffered a downhill slide in the U.S., the company's sales in Europe are excellent: they are the top-selling computer in several markets. Since the company sells essentially the same machines in Europe as it does in the U.S., reasons for the remarkable difference in European and U.S. sales appear to lie in the way the computers were marketed and in the follow-up support that was provided (or not provided). Many personnel changes at top levels in the U.S. company have not helped. Commodore agrees with the conclusion that U.S. marketing is a problem; it revamped its U.S. marketing and dealer support system in 1981. Since then their sales have increased dramatically, but they still do not compete well, in terms of units sold, with Apple, Radio Shack, and probably Atari. Commodore does, however, sell the widest range of computers available from one company. Commodore's computers begin with an $88 VIC that is just a few steps up from a video game machine and go all the way up to very powerful business computers with hard disk systems. Commodore recently announced several new models which will be reviewed here. Some of the older, more established models will also be reviewed. Our review of the new models, however, is based on limited knowledge of the machines. (It is quite difficult to get information from Commodore.)

The VIC-20

Video Display. The VIC connects to your color television and displays 22 lines of 23 characters, upper and lower case. That means you can only have a maximum of 506 characters on the screen at once. Color graphics on the VIC are good (but not great).

Keyboard. The $299 VIC uses a standard-size, typewriter-style keyboard. To our knowledge, it is the least expensive computer with a standard keyboard. The VIC has a good keyboard, particularly when you consider that keyboards alone on some business machines cost over $200. There are even four programmable function keys.

RAM. 5K of RAM is standard; the VIC can use up to 32K.

Languages Used. The VIC has a good version of BASIC in ROM that is similar to the BASIC used in the more expensive Commodore computers. Programs written for the PET computer should generally run on the VIC if they can deal with the 23-character display-line length (the PET uses 40-character lines). PILOT is also available from a non-Commodore source.

Storage. The VIC uses the standard Commodore cassette unit or a 5¼-inch disk drive. Both are optional.

Software. Commodore sells software for the VIC in two media formats. There are game cartridges that can be plugged into a slot in the back of the computer, and there are programs available on cassette tape. The tape system is relatively reliable. Although software for the VIC was scarce in 1981 and early 1982, there is now a healthy supply of software available. While much of the software for the VIC consists of games, there are a number of educational programs and home financial and small business programs.

I/O Ports. The computer can be connected to joysticks and game paddles. A serial port is also included. The VIC is capable of generating all sorts of sounds through your television speaker.

Service. Local Commodore dealers can generally provide some service for the VIC. Since it is also sold in some discount and department stores, you may find it necessary to mail it into regional repair centers for service. Our experience with the VIC indicates a heat-related problem in the computer (at least in the ones we used). The computer may work well for half an hour or more and then behave erratically or stop working altogether as heat inside the case builds up. Commodore should be able to correct this fairly easily. The VIC is a lot of computer for $88. It can be used as a game machine, with many game cartridges available. In addition, it will be a good first computer for many students and adults since it has a good standard BASIC and uses a regular keyboard. Many companies make accessories for the VIC.

PET 4016/4032

These are the standard PET computers which have been on the market for several years.

Video Display. These computers come with a 12-inch green screen built-in monitor and a 25 by 40 display. They display both upper and lower-case characters. The display is crisp, and the computer has good low-resolution graphics.

Keyboard. There are two versions of the PET keyboard currently in production. They have a standard size and format, and both have numeric keypads. One version prints letters in capitals in the unshifted mode and graphics symbols in the shifted mode. The other prints lower case letters when the shift key is not pressed and capital letters when it is—the same format as a standard typewriter. You can switch from one keyboard version to the other with one simple instruction. Overall, they are good quality keyboards.

RAM. The 4016 had 16K of user RAM; the 4032 has 32K. It is possible to *upgrade* a 16K machine to 32K but not as easily as you can on a TRS-80 Model III or Apple II. Even if you use the PET with disk drives the entire 16 or 32K is available for you to use since the Commodore computers use *intelligent* disk systems that do not require you to load disk operating system software into RAM before using disks. That means a 32K PET will have as much or more user-available memory than many computers with 48K of RAM and disk systems that require a DOS.

Languages Used. The PET computers use a ROM version of Microsoft BASIC. Version 4.0 BASIC is used in all the Commodore computers above the level of the Model 64. Many other languages are available for the PET from third-party suppliers.

Storage. All Commodore computers can store data on the Commodore cassette recorder. It retails for approximately $75 and is usually reliable. There are also several disk systems available which range from a single disk drive that stores 170K on each diskette (5¼-inch) to a double-sided dual disk unit that is capable of storing over a million bytes on each diskette. Two hard disk systems with 5 million and 7.5 million bytes capacity have been announced but few, if any, had been delivered to dealers at the time of this writing.

The disk drives in Commodore computers are, in our opinion, one of their strongest features. The more expensive models store four to eight times as much data as the standard drive units currently offered on most small computers, and they do their job very reliably. Commodore builds the disk instructions into its BASIC, making the drives very convenient to use.

Software. Although there is not as much software available for the PET as for the Apple and TRS-80 Model III, our guess is that the amount available for the PET puts it third or fourth in quantity available (the ATARI 800/400 is at about the same level). There are many educational programs for the PET and you should have your choice of at least three or four different programs if you want software for typical business, home or professional applications.

I/O Ports. The PETs use the IEEE-488 standard for connecting printers, disk drives, and other accessories. This is good because the quality of data transfer is high when this standard is used; but it is bad because many manufacturers of accessories sell parallel and serial versions of their products, but not IEEE-488 versions. Consequently you may be limited to printers and other accessories supplied by Commodore. However, serial and parallel converters are carried by most Commodore dealers and cost between $100 and $175.

One more comment about the Commodore 499 interface.

PET 4032

Apparently Commodore did not follow all the standards specified by IEEE-488, thus equipment designed for other computers (e.g., Hewlett-Packard) that expect a completely faithful rendition of the 488 standard may not always work properly on Commodore computers.

The Commodore 64

Announced in early 1982, the 64 has been slow getting into the stores. (Commodore, in fact, has a history of announcing products well before they are actually available for sale.)

The 64 looks a lot like the VIC. Their keyboards look identical. The 64 can use many of the peripherals developed for the VIC. However, the 64 retails for under $400. For that you get all the display, sound, game, and color graphics features, and the ability to use VIC accessories. You get 64K of RAM, although there is only 39K of user-available RAM in BASIC and 52K available in machine language.

The 64 is advertised as being CP/M compatible since owners can purchase a card that lets you add a Z80 microprocessor. That sounds fine, but CP/M compatibility is more than having a Z80 chip in the system. Most CP/M software expects to run on a computer with a 24- or 25-line by 80-character display, while the 64 has a 25 by 40 format. The 64 may not be as compatible with CP/M as Commodore claims. The 64 has a PET emulator that will allow you to run the many programs available for the PET computer series.

Commodore 64

Commodore plans to release a large number of programs this year for the 64 computer. Some will be sophisticated business programs, others will be game and educational programs. The 64 will compete feature for feature with computers already on the market that cost much more.

CBM 8032 and Super PET

Commodore's 8032 computer is really no more than a 4032 with a 25-line by 80-column display. The 8032 uses the same accessories and the same IEEE-488 interconnection standard; it can even run in the 40-column mode if necessary. The 8032 is aimed primarily at the business market where 80 characters on a line is a desirable, if not necessary, feature.

The SuperPET is an 8032 with extra memory, a second microprocessor chip, and a whole series of computer languages which were developed at the University of Waterloo in Canada.

The Waterloo languages are primarily teaching languages since they give the user more detailed information on what is wrong with a program than most standard languages. All this help, however, takes up quite a bit of memory, which is why Commodore increased the RAM in the SuperPET to 96K. The SuperPET is rarely found in business. It is most at home in high school and university computer programming classes.

The P, B, and BX Series Computers

In May, 1982, at the National Computing Conference, Commodore announced a new line of computers. Designated the P, B, and BX series they appear to be replacements for the PET 4016/32 and CBM 8032 computers (although this came as a surprise to some of Commodore's dealers).

Commodore P128   Commodore B series

The computers are housed in sleek, sculpted, plastic cases and have full-size typewriter-style keyboards with a number of programmable function keys. The P128 computer, which should retail for around $700, connects to your color television, uses a 25 by 40 display with color graphics, and has 128K of RAM. The computer has a maximum RAM capacity of over 800K, a game cartridge slot, sound, and very good color graphics. Although it still has the IEEE-488 interface, the computer also has a serial interface for connecting modems and printers.

The B and BX series computers come with a green screen monitor and display 25 lines of 80 characters. All three series use an excellent keyboard with numeric keypad and several programmable function keys. The B and BX computers have graphics similar to the current PET series (not color graphics like the model 64). A serial port is standard. The B series has a minumum of 128K RAM; the BX series has at least 256K. Both have a maximum RAM capacity of 896K. The BASIC on all the new computers is Version 4.0. Both B and BX series have two built-in 5¼-inch disk drives, and both have optional circuit cards that let you run CP/M software.

ATARI COMPUTERS

At the 1983 Consumer Electonics Show in Chicago ATARI announced the replacement of its 800 and 400 models with four new computers. ATARI, while it has enjoyed some success in the personal computer market, has not come to dominate the field. They hope the new series will do just that. All four models are software-compatible with the older 800 and 400 models. That means thousands of programs are available for these new models.

Video Display. Twenty-four lines of 40 characters, upper and lower case, and excellent color graphics are features of these systems. The ATARI computers use a color television or color monitor for display. They can generate a range of sounds through the television speaker. The ATARI machines have 5 different text *modes* and 11 graphics *modes*. That means you have a choice of the type of text (e.g. big letters, small letters) and graphics (e.g. very fine, precise graphics or coarser, easier to program graphics).

Keyboard. All the ATARI computers use a standard typewriter layout. The ATARI keyboards have an excellent feel to them and incorporate several special keys (e.g. a HELP key). The 600 and 800 models have 62 keypads on their keyboards, the 1400 and 1450 have 66. None of the models have separate numeric keypads, however.

RAM. The 600 has 16K of RAM and is expandable to 64K. The other models have 64K standard.

Languages Used. The computers can be programmed in a version of BASIC that is unique to ATARI. A Microsoft BASIC should be available ,as an option for all the models. In addition, ATARI has a very good PILOT and a special version of Logo for their computers.

Software. There are thousands of recreational and educational programs for this computer with more appearing each month. Many games are available in cartridges, and software is also on cassette and diskette. ATARI probably ranks third or fourth in quantity of software available. ATARI has announced a CP/M module for their computers that makes it possible to run many of the business and professional programs available only in CP/M versions on an ATARI computer. The CP/M module contains a completely different microprocessor (Z80) than the one used in the computer (6502), as well as 64K of RAM. In addition, the system includes provision for operating in either 40- or 80-character-per-line formats. The ability to run in an 80-column format is important because most of the software written for CP/M computers expects the computer to handle 80 characters per line.

Storage. The computers have standard cassette storage facilities that work reliably. However, the cassette recorder itself is not included in the price, and you must use the ATARI recorder.

Optional 5¼ inch disk drives are also available. The 1450 model comes with one double-sided, dual-density disk drive as standard equipment. It can store 254K on each diskette. Disk drives for the 600 and 800 computers are single-sided and store 127K on each diskette. Current disk drives for the ATARI computers operate much faster than the ones used with earlier models.

I/O Ports. There are provisions for connecting light pens, joysticks, game controllers, and serial printers and modems. The 1400 and 1450 models have a built-in modem and a voice synthesizer that lets the computer talk to you.

ATARI is making a strong run at the home and educational segments of the personal computer market. The 600, at $199 retail, is likely to be a very popular computer. Prices for the other three ATARI computers had not been announced when this was written. Price, however, is likely to be the determining factor in the popularity of these computers. They have outstanding features for home and educational use—excellent color graphics, sound synthesis, lots of good software, and easy to use keyboards. If the price is right, they will be very popular. The computers are even likely to find their place on the desks of many professional and business users. ATARI has several good programs for tasks such as word processing, investment analysis, and business record-keeping. Service is widely available for the computers through authorized service centers.

ATARI also has a significant number of accessories for their computers. Their $350 letter-quality printer is the least expensive method we know of to get typewriter quality printouts from a computer.

COLECO ADAM

Coleco, a well-known toy company that markets a popular video game called ColecoVision, caught the attention of many experts in the personal computer field when it announced its new computer system, ADAM, at the Consumer Electronics Show in the summer of 1983. The computer will not be available in stores until the end of 1983, but insiders already consider it a likely winner in the under-$1000 market. Why was so much attention given to a computer that is the first offering of a toy company? In one word, price. Coleco announced the computer would retail for around $600. That price will include some surprising items. You get a computer with 80K of RAM, BASIC in ROM, color graphics and sound synthesis, and a full-size, high-quality keyboard. The computer will also run all the video games available for the ColecoVision video game and has connections for game paddles and joysticks. The computer also comes with *bundled software* including a word processor and electronic spread sheet. That is quite a bit for $600, but we're not through yet. The price also includes a daisy wheel printer and a mass storage system that is faster and more reliable than cassette systems, but not quite as flexible as a disk drive. Until Coleco announced ADAM the cheapest daisy wheel printer on the market had a list price of over $600. Offering this much equipment for $600 brings the price/performance ratio of personal computers to a new level.

There are, of course, some questions to be answered. Can Coleco manufacture the computer in quantity? Will it operate reliably? Will software be readily available? Is it as easy to use as it appears? If these questions are answered positively and if other manufacturers resist the temptation to drastically cut prices on their models, Coleco will be a name to reckon with in the home and educational computer market.

THE TIMEX SINCLAIR 1000 AND THE SINCLAIR ZX81

The Sinclair ZX81 was designed by Sinclair Research Ltd. of Cambridge, England, and built by Timex in a plant in Scotland. Timex is now marketing its own version of the computer, the Timex Sinclair 1000.

Video Display. This marvelous little midget computer displays 24 lines of 32 characters on your black and white television. The computer can display graphics similar to those available on the PET computer.

Keyboard. The small, touch-sensitive, plastic membrane keyboard is arranged in the same format as a typewriter keyboard, only smaller. Similar keyboards beep when you press each keypad. This one doesn't; the only way you know that a keypress has been registered is to look at the screen. The keyboard is probably the weakest feature of this computer, but it is one reason why the Sinclair can be sold at such a low price (around $50).

RAM. 1K of RAM is standard on the older ZX81 version; 2K is standard on the 1000. Up to 64K can be added.

Languages Used. BASIC is provided in ROM. The standard BASIC used in the computer is not Microsoft-compatible, but it is a very good BASIC. It helps the beginning programmer by refusing to enter a line of instructions if it contains an error. It even marks the point in the line where the error occurs.

Storage. The computer uses standard cassette recorders for storage.

Software. There are many programs for this computer. The magazine, *SYNC*, published by Creative Computing Press, is devoted to the Sinclair computers. Many programs are advertised in it.

I/O Ports. Sinclair sells a small dot-matrix printer ($100)

Timex Sinclair 1000

that can be used with the computer. Other companies sell a variety of interface devices that permit you to connect it to modems, printers, and home control units.

Service. There is a mail-in repair service for these computers. No local service is available. Our understanding is that defective units are often exchanged for new ones.

Clive Sinclair reports that Sinclair Research Ltd. has sold over 900,000 of the Timex Sinclair 1000 and its predecessors, the ZX80 and the ZX81. Even at the low price, that is a lot of computers. What do you get for your money? Well, it isn't an IBM 370 but it is a real computer that speaks BASIC. The keyboard is hard to use, but what do you expect for $50? Several companies do a brisk business in keyboard conversion kits for the Sinclair. It is not difficult to add a full-size keyboard to the computer.

The 1000 is small enough to be carried in a purse or briefcase. You may feel a little chagrined when someone plops their ATARI computer or Radio Shack TRS-80 Model IV down beside it, but the 1000 is one of the cheapest ways to get started with small computers.

TIMEX SINCLAIR 1500

Although the Timex Sinclair 1000 is very popular—over a million have been sold—there is a virtually universal complaint about it. The keyboard is hard to use. The Timex Sinclair 1500 is essentially a TS1000 with a better keyboard and 16K of RAM built in. It retails for $80 and is recommended over the TS100 because of the improved keyboard and extra memory. RAM can be expanded to 32K in this computer, and there are provisions for plugging in cartridges that contain programs in ROM. Most of the software available for the TS1000 will run on the TS1500.

THE TIMEX SINCLAIR 2000

This is another computer that emerged from the research laboratories of Sinclair Research in England. With 48K of RAM the 2000 will retail for $200; with 16K of RAM it is priced at $150. The computer uses the same type of BASIC and the same method of entering programs as the TS1000 and TS1500. There are, however, a number of enhancements. The display is 24 lines of 32 or 64 characters, and there are provisions for color graphics and sound synthesis. The keyboard has also been improved. It consists of separate keys rather than the plastic membrane used on the TS1000. The TS2000's BASIC is surprisingly sophisticated. It is better than the BASICs supplied on several more expensive computers and has a number of keywords that make using the color graphics and sound features easier than on computers such as the VIC from Commodore.

The TS2000 is similar to the Sinclair Spectrum, which is sold only outside the U.S. by Sinclair Research. Both computers offer a quite a bit of computing power for the price.

THE TI 99/4A

Video Display. This computer uses your color television (or a color monitor) as its display unit. It puts 24 lines of 32 characters on the screen, upper case only. The color graphics on the TI computer are very good, but they do not compensate for the small number of characters displayed on each line. Sound is built-in.

Keyboard. The original TI 99/4 computer had a calculator-style keyboard that was criticized by virtually everyone. Now the 99/4A has a keyboard that looks like a standard typewriter-style unit, but isn't. It is several inches narrower than keyboards on other small computers. It appears that when TI redesigned their keyboard, they required their engineers to make it fit in the same space as the older keyboard so they wouldn't have to redesign the computer's case. The result is that many standard typewriter characters can only be typed with the function key depressed. The keyboard is still difficult to use. The keyboard and the video display capacity are major drawbacks.

Languages Used. BASIC is in ROM and another, more powerful, BASIC is an extra-cost option. In addition, TI offers their own version of the Logo language for this computer. In our opinion it is one of the best implementations of Logo currently on the market. If you have small children, the quality of the Logo language may be enough to outweigh the computer's shortcomings in other areas. Several other languages are also available.

RAM. 16K is standard; it can be expanded to 72K.

Storage. The standard computer will store data on a cassette recorder. A 5¼-inch disk drive system is optional. Around 90K can be stored on each diskette.

Software. There is a fair amount of software available for the TI computer, but not as much as you will find for some of the front runners such as Apple, Radio Shack, ATARI and Commodore. TI is particularly strong in the area of early childhood learning and in educational software for elementary school children. In other areas the supply is limited. Software is available in ROM cartridges, on tape and on diskette. The magazine

99er concentrates on the TI 99/4A and carries ads for lots of software.

I/O Ports. There is a serial port, and ports for game paddle/joystick connections. Current versions use an optional expansion chassis to house accessories such as the speech synthesizer.

Service. TI has a mail-in repair service for this computer. In some large cities you may be able to deliver your computer to a repair center. TI has a very good reputation for repair service.

Texas Instruments TI99

Although the TI 99/4A has been on the market for several years, it has never been a popular system. The company alienated many independent programmers during the first year the computer was available by making it difficult for non-TI programmers to write commercial software for the computer. The company decided that TI could supply all the software and make all the profit. That decision proved to be disastrous because lack of software was a major problem for a long time. Although TI is more helpful today, the dampening of that early enthusiasm from third party programmers definitely hurt TI.

TI dropped the price of the computer several times over the years; it now costs hundreds of dollars less than it did when it was first announced. The low price and its availability in discount stores has helped increase sales. Display capacity and keyboard are weak points; TI Logo is a strong point.

THE OSBORNE I

The Osborne I computer has been a fantastic hit. It is a portable computer that latches up like a briefcase.

Video Display. This computer uses a self-contained 5-inch black and white display that is too small and too fuzzy for our tastes. It displays 24 lines of 52 characters. If you are using a program that expects an 80-character line, the Osborne I shifts the display to show a 52-character *window*. That is, it scrolls horizontally as well as vertically. A larger, optional monitor is also available.

Keyboard. The computer has a standard, full-size typewriter-style keyboard of good quality. A numeric keypad is included.

RAM. 64K is standard. You must load the CP/M operating system and the language you are using into RAM. Whatever is left over is available for your use.

Languages. The computer comes with CBASIC and MBASIC, two very good business-oriented programming languages. Many others are available since the computer is CP/M compatible. CP/M, in fact, is included in the price of the computer.

Storage. Two single-density 5¼-inch disk drives are built-in. They store 100K on each diskette. A double-density disk system has been announced, but its appearance on the market has been delayed several times.

Software. This is an unusual feature in a computer that is itself unusual. The computer comes with a very sophisticated word processing program (Wordstar), an excellent spreadsheet program (SuperCalc), and a mailing list program (Mailmerge). If you add up the retail prices of all the software provided with the computer (including CP/M and the two BASICs) the cost of the software alone comes close to the price of the computer. Since the computer is CP/M compatible, there is a great deal of software available for it.

I/O Ports. The computer includes serial, parallel, and IEEE-488 interfaces.

Service. We do not have any direct knowledge of the service provided. Some dealers are able to handle most problems. The factory has had some problems responding to customer needs

Osborne I Computer

because so many of the computers have been sold in so short a time.

Adam Osborne, president of Osborne Computer Company, has been a writer, lecturer, and all-around critic of computer manufacturers for many years. His acid-tipped pen (actually word processor) has taken the majority of manufacturers sternly to task. Now that he has his own shop, many in the industry have taken private and public delight each time he experienced the same problems other companies faced. There have, indeed, been problems at Osborne, but had the owner not been Adam Osborne, they probably would have been considered no more than average for a new computer company.

The price, the software that comes with it, and the portability of the Osborne I all make it a very attractive computer for people who travel and want to take their computer with them. Drawbacks are the single density disk drives, the small display screen, and the 52-character lines. However, those limitations are not enough to discourage thousands from ordering the first inexpensive, business-oriented briefcase computer.

In the summer of 1983 Osborne announced a new computer, the Osborne Executive. It is similar to the Osborne I in concept and design but deals very nicely with the feature most criticized on the I—the small, fuzzy display. The new Osborne II has a 7″ amber screen that displays 24 clear, crisp lines of 80 characters. Although it is hundreds of dollars higher in price than the I, it is likely to be considered a replacement for the I because the display on the I is so weak. Osborne has also announced an optional circuit board for the Executive that lets you run software written for the very popular IBM PC. Although the extra card puts the price of the Executive well over $3000, it is expected to sell well because portability is increasingly considered desirable and also because Osborne spends millions on advertising their computers and have thus achieved name recognition while manufacturers of similar, lower-priced computers have not.

THE KAYPRO II

This computer has been called a clone of the Osborne I since it too is a portable, briefcase-style system that comes with CP/M and a set of business software (word processor and spread sheet) as well as SBASIC, another BASIC for business applications. The price is the same as the price of an Osborne I. The package of software included with this computer is not

Kaypro II

as well-known, nor as popular, as the Osborne software package. On the other hand, the disk drives of the Kaypro II are double density (200K per diskette), and the built-in video monitor is 9 inches rather than 5 inches. The Kaypro is thus able to display a full 24 lines of 80 characters. The Kaypro has both serial and parallel ports.

The Osborne I is better known than the Kaypro, and it has superior software. The Kaypro II has superior features, but it is made by a company that is not yet well-established in the small computer field. At present it has a limited dealer network. However, the Kaypro II has the potential to become an excellent, portable, business computer.

GRID Compass

THE OTRONA AND GRID COMPUTERS

Two other computers, the Otrona Attache and the Grid Compass, are also entering the specialized *briefcase-size* computer market.

The Otrona Attache is a very well-constructed briefcase computer weighing less than 17 pounds (the Osborne I is 24 pounds, the Kaypro II just over 24). It has double-density, double-sided disk drives (380K per diskette) and the CP/M disk operating system.

The Otrona has a 5-inch built-in high-resolution green screen monitor. The $4000 price tag on the Otrona Attache puts it in an entirely different price class than the Osborne and Kaypro computers.

Even $4000 is not enough to buy the Compass computer from Grid Systems Corporation. The 9.5 pound Compass has a futuristic flat screen display and uses one of the newer, faster microprocessor chips. The Compass has 256K of RAM memory *and* 256K of bubble memory (it doesn't lose the data stored in it when the power is turned off). The computer, priced at $8150, is intended for well-heeled executives who want not only computing power on their desk, but also a computer they can use to communicate with mainframe computers. The company built a modem into the computer and supports a nationwide computer data storage system that is accessible from any telephone.

The Compass is too small to really be called a briefcase computer; it fits inside a standard briefcase with plenty of room left over. The Compass will have a limited market because of its price and software availability.

THE IBM PC

Video Display. This computer displays 25 lines of 80 characters and has a wide range of excellent graphics features. IBM gives you the option of using either a black and white (monochrome) or a color monitor. The computer can be connected to anything from a $100 black and white television to a $1000 RGB (red, green, blue) color monitor. With an expensive color monitor the IBM computer is capable of beautiful graphics, some of the best available with a small computer.

Keyboard. The IBM PC keyboard is good but the keys are oddly placed. There are 10 programmable function keys and a numeric keypad.

RAM. The computer has 16K in the minimal system. IBM and other vendors supply plug-in cards so it can be expanded to 512K. Although the computer is relatively new, there are literally hundreds of companies making all sorts of accessory cards that plug into the IBM PC, often at prices considerably lower than the retail IBM price for an equivalent product.

Languages Used. BASIC is standard while at least six or seven other languages (including enhanced versions of BASIC) are available as options. In addition, there are several versions of CP/M, and two other disk operating systems available. The IBM PC is attractive to programmers because there are so many good languages to use.

IBM Personal Computer

Storage. There is room in the computer's case for two 5¼-inch disk drives. They are double-density, single-sided drives that store 160K on each diskette. Two additional drives can be added outside the case. Many companies sell IBM PC-compatible drives. Several have hard disk drives that fit right into the case where a floppy disk drive would normally be placed.

I/O Ports. A cassette storage interface is standard, everything else is optional. You can buy an interface card that lets you connect virtually anything any other computer uses. There are so many alternatives and options, it is difficult to figure out just what you want.

Software. This is a new computer, but there are already hundreds, perhaps thousands, of programs available for it in

most categories. Currently, the computer has fewer game and
educational programs than several other systems, but it has a
large amount of business software. After some initial difficulties with the contracts IBM offered to independent software
developers, the company is moving full speed toward a huge
line of IBM software. At the same time, many programmers
are writing software for the IBM PC because it is perceived
as a sure winner in the popularity race. And because there are
so many programmers writing software for the PC, it is likely
to be a successful computer, a good example of a self-fulfilling
prophecy.

Service. Before being awarded a dealership, a store must
set up and qualify as a service center. Since IBM does not
allow its dealers to sell by mail, you should be able to get
service from the same place that sold you the computer.

The IBM PC gets an "A" in virtually every category except
the keyboard. What IBM doesn't supply, someone else does.
The computer looks good, works well, and has excellent documentation. Although the price of this computer is higher than
comparable units from several other companies, it is not *that*
much higher. The cost of a complete system can be reduced
if you buy some of the accessories and expansion cards from
non-IBM sources.

EAGLE PC

The popularity of the IBM PC caught many people in the
business off-guard. Many of us did not expect the mainframe
computer giant to capture so much of the market so quickly.
The popularity of the IBM PC is probably due to three main
reasons—it is a reliable, reasonably well designed product; it
is made by a company that has a strong reputation for quality
and service in the mind of the buying public; and IBM is
spending millions of dollars on advertising.

The current state of the small computer market is such that
smaller companies with new computers have difficulty getting
a share of the market even when their products offer good value
for the money. One effective method of breaking into the small

computer market, however, is to design a computer that is software and/or hardware compatible with an existing computer. Several computer companies—including Columbia, Hyperion, Eagle, Sequa, and Compaq—manufacture computers which are supposed to be *IBM compatible*. That is, a piece of software written for the IBM PC should run, without modification, on the other computer.

Complete, 100 percent compatibility with the IBM PC is extremely difficult, if not impossible, to achieve. Several manufacturers, however, have a remarkable degree of compatibility. The portable computer developed by Compaq, for example, is probably 95 percent compatible.

The Eagle Computer Corporation, with its Eagle PC, has also achieved over 90 percent compatibility. Their computer even looks like the IBM PC. Various models of the Eagle PC retail for between $2000 (64K RAM, one disk drive, no monitor, no software) and $4495 (128K RAM, one disk drive, monitor, one 10-million-byte hard disk, and a set of software that includes an excellent word processor and spread sheet as well as MSDOS and CPM86). The most popular model is the PC-2, which retails for $3495. It has 128K RAM, two disk drives which store 320K on each diskette, a monitor, and a package of software.

Although the Eagle runs most of the software written for the IBM PC, the Eagle costs hundreds of dollars less than a similarly equipped IBM PC. The Eagle is, we feel, superior to the IBM in some areas. The Eagle keyboard, for example, has 24 programmable function keys arranged across the top of the keyboard and at the bottom right. There is a separate numeric keypad *and* a set of four cursor control keys. In addition, the keyboard is arranged in the same format as an IBM Selectric keyboard. The RETURN and SHIFT keys are where you expect them to be. The IBM PC keyboard put the cursor control keys on the numeric keypad and placed the RETURN and SHIFT keys in awkward locations. The Eagle PC-2 has two serial ports, one parallel port, a video port and high-quality green screen monitor, and software that retails for over $1000. All that is *optional* on the IBM PC and must be purchased at extra cost. The extra value you get when you buy an Eagle PC should help compensate for the lack of name recognition for the Eagle.

XEROX 820

Xerox is, of course, well-known by virtue of its dominance in the copier market. Xerox now has several office-automation products in addition to their extensive line of copiers.

Xerox 820

The Xerox 820 computer came out at about the same time as the IBM PC, and many expected the two to be compared. For the most part, such comparison was to the detriment of Xerox. While IBM spent millions on the design and development of their computer, Xerox bought the rights to a computer known as the *Ferguson Big Board* and turned it into the Xerox 820. The Big Board computer is a kit computer that is sold through the mail. It is popular because it provides the builder with a 64K RAM, CP/M compatible computer at a reasonable price. It is a plain, no frills system.

The Xerox 820 is a plain, no frills system. It retails for $2995, has two 5¼-inch disk drives (92K per diskette), has a 24 by 80 black and white 12-inch display (no graphics, no color), and runs CP/M as its only operating system. It can also use 8-inch disk drives which are optional.

This no-frills computer is not a bad one; it just isn't a great one. The price isn't spectacular and the features aren't exciting. It doesn't seem to belong in the Xerox stable. If the price were reduced to $1400, the 820 might be attractive to those who need a CP/M computer with a full screen display. Otherwise, it is not competitive with other machines in its price range (e.g., the Eagle II).

NORTHSTAR ADVANTAGE

Video Display. A built-in 12-inch green screen monitor displays 24 lines of 80 characters. The Advantage has some of the best graphics features available on a small-business computer.

Keyboard. The Advantage has a very good, standard-size keyboard with 15 programmable function keys and a numeric keypad.

RAM. 64K RAM is standard.

Languages Used. NorthStar provides several operating systems and BASICs for the Advantage, including an enhanced version of CP/M. Good language and disk operating system software are characteristic of NorthStar computers.

NorthStar Advantage

Storage. There are two built-in double-sided double density 5¼-inch disk drives. They store 360K on each diskette. Hard disk drives are also available.

Software. NorthStar itself sells a wide range of business software for its computers, and many CP/M compatible programs will run on the Advantage. It is not a game/recreational computer; few game programs are available.

I/O Ports. The Advantage has several expansion slots that use *S-100* circuit boards. This type of computer board is made by many companies. You can buy add-on boards from NorthStar or from other suppliers. Parallel and serial ports do not come with the computer; you must buy them separately.

Service. NorthStar dealers generally provide service on the Advantage.

NorthStar has been in business since the first years of the microcomputer revolution. It now specializes in moderate to high-priced business-oriented computers of high quality. Many programmers use NorthStar computers because of their quality and dependability. If you are shopping for a solid business computer, this one deserves your attention.

New Models (and Sleepers)

This section covers a number of computers that have recently been placed on the market, such as the EPSON HX-20 and the DEC Rainbow, as well as a few models that have been around for a while but have been only moderately successful. There may be a future Apple II in this group, but it is too early to tell. The descriptions and comments on these computers are less detailed because they are new and untried.

EAGLE II

The Eagle II is one of a series of computers recently announced by Eagle Computer Company, a company better known for computer-controlled audio-visual equipment. All the models are similar in design to the TRS-80 Model III and the NorthStar Advantage. There is one case which contains the keyboard, a 12-inch green screen monitor (24 by 80) and two disk drives. (On the Eagle IV and V one of the disk drives is a hard disk drive with 7.5 or 15 million bytes of storage.) The two 5¼-inch disk drives hold 390K on each diskette.

The computer retails for $1995, an excellent price when you learn that a very good word processing program, an electronic spreadsheet program, and CP/M plus BASIC are included in the price. The computer is priced much lower than comparable models with equivalent software.

Eagle II

The Eagle II looks good; it is easy to use; and it can run standard CP/M software. It should be a competitive computer in the small business market. Two major problems are the lack of name recognition in the computer field and the absence of a large dealer network.

EPSON HX-20

This is an unusual computer. It has a standard-size keyboard, but it is considered a portable computer because it runs on either batteries or wall current. It contains its own display, a tiny cassette recorder and even a printer. The display is a *liquid crystal* type with a capacity for 4 lines of 20 characters each. The printer can print 24 characters per line on adding machine-size paper. There is a serial interface, 16K of RAM (maximum of 32K possible), and a powerful version of Microsoft BASIC in ROM.

This computer will retail for around $750 and is made by

the company that dominates the low-cost dot-matrix printer market with their Epson MX-80 series of printers. It has provisions for a bar code reader, memory that doesn't lose its data when the power is switched off, and the ability to use full-size cassette recorders for storage. We can't quite figure out just who is going to buy this machine and what they will do with it, but it is a cute little fella!

Epson HX-20

THE DEC RAINBOW 100

Digital Equipment Corporation is one of the best-known manufacturers of minicomputers. It is also the second largest computer manufacturer in the world. DEC's popular minicomputer, the PDP-11, is used in thousands of businesses, universities, and research laboratories today. The success of their minis may be one reason why DEC did not move into the personal computing market until 1982.

DEC announced four new computers at the National Computer Conference in June 1982. All share the same keyboard and 12-inch monitor. The more expensive units, however, use a version of the PDP-11 processor and the intermediate unit has a version of the PDP-8 processor. We will describe the least expensive unit here, the Rainbow 100.

There are several surprises in the Rainbow 100. First, it uses rather odd disk drives. They use 5¼-inch diskettes, but store 400K on each one, *and* you can insert two diskettes in each drive. Thus you have 800K of storage on the standard drive and another 800K if you buy the optional second drive. Both fit inside the chassis.

The keyboard is another high performance item. It has a total of 103 keys (compared to 48 for the TI 99/4A, 65 for the TRS-80 Model III and 51 for the Apple II). There are 36 different function keys, many of which can be user-programmed. The keyboard appears to be as good or better than the keyboard on the IBM PC.

The video display is also different. It will display 24 lines of 80 characters as will most computers aimed at the business market. However, the Rainbow 100 will also display 24 lines of 132 characters! Color graphics are an extra-cost option.

Finally, the computer is CP/M compatible, but with a twist. There are currently two popular versions of CP/M, Version 2.2 for computers that use the older and slower Z80 microprocessor chip and Version 86 for computers using the newer, faster 8086/8088 chip. The Z80 chip is an *8-bit* chip; the 8086 and 8088 are *16-bit* chips. The difference in design allows the 8086 to do its work much faster. Instead of making a choice between the two microprocessors, DEC put both a Z80 chip and an 8086 chip in the Rainbow 100. Its version of CP/M checks to see if it is running a 2.2 compatible program or a CP/M-86 compatible program and adjusts automatically. This feature will make a DEC computer very attractive to customers who want a business or professional computer with lots of software. DEC has also developed its own software for the computer, but we have not had an opportunity to work with it. The computer comes with 64K of RAM which can be upgraded to 256K. A serial port is standard.

NEC PC-8000

NEC is the manufacturer of a popular letter-quality printer, the Spinwriter. It also builds several computers that are popular in the Japanese small-computer market. The NEC 8000 computer is a model that has a number of premium features, such as good color graphics, sound synthesis, a keyboard with programmable function keys, and a numeric keypad. The computer is being marketed as a business and a personal computer.

Some software is available for it in all major areas of application.

There are three parts to a full system—a keyboard unit, an expansion unit and a dual disk drive unit. The retail price of the keyboard is $1295. You can add a monitor or TV to it and a tape recorder, and be in business. The expansion unit lets you put in more memory and provides several I/O ports. If you want to add disk drives, you must buy the expansion unit. The dual disk unit itself is another $1295.

NEC 8000

Although the unit does offer some desirable features, the price of a complete system, almost $3400 if purchased at the retail price, seems steep. It does have a CP/M option, and if you use an RGB color monitor, the graphics are outstanding. The BASIC in ROM is a very good version of Microsoft BASIC.

Other Computers of Interest

There is simply not enough space to describe in detail all of the models that suit the computing needs and interests of first-time computer buyers. This final section briefly examines some of the companies and computers not already considered.

CROMEMCO

A respected manufacturer of business computers, Cromemco has a complete line of high quality computers. Cromemco has been around almost as long as small computers have.

HEATH/ZENITH

Heath, known for its superb electronic kits, was purchased by Zenith about three years ago. The desktop, disk-based computer from Heath has a built-in video monitor, keyboard, and disk drive. It is sold as the H-89 and the Z-89, depending on whether Heath or Zenith sells it. The Heath-89 sells for $1995 with one 5¼-inch floppy disk drive. Heath also sells several other models. It has an active users group and a large library of software for their computers. The 89 is CP/M compatible. It is worth looking into, especially if there is a local dealer that provides support and service.

HEWLETT PACKARD

HP makes several different computers, most of them desktop models used primarily by engineers and scientists. The HP computers are not strong sellers outside that population of owners. They have a reputation for high quality, high price and features that appeal to the engineering professional.

TELEVIDEO

This company manufactures good terminals. In 1982, they began marketing a computer as well. It is similar to both the NorthStar Advantage and the Eagle II, costs $3495, has a well-designed case and features superior editing features and a high-quality 12-inch built-in display.

VECTOR GRAPHIC

Like Cromemco, Vector Graphic is an established manu-facturer of small business computers. Vector Graphic computers are known for their quality. Several different models are available.

VICTOR 9000

The Victor company is best-known for its cash registers and calculators. The Victor 9000 computer, an excellent system, was not designed by Victor but by Sirius, a company controlled by Chuck Peddle, one of the movers and shakers in the development of the Commodore PET. Although Victor put its name on most of the computer's business software (e.g., Victorcalc), most of it seems to be software that is available for other computers under more familiar names.

CHAPTER 11

Computer Peripherals

The ad for the new computer may prominently display a price that looks good. It may be $295, $595, or $1295. The price quoted, however, may not tell the whole story. Some manufacturers quote prices for complete systems—everything you need to get started. However, prices quoted by other manufacturers may not include some of the necessary equipment or accessories.

Jerry's first computer cost $995. It was a kit containing at least 20,000 parts. (At least, it seemed like 20,000 before it was assembled.) As it turned out, the $995 did not cover everything needed to get the computer working. He spent $65 on a tape recorder, $150 on a monitor, $600 for 16K of memory and $75 for BASIC. The $995 computer actually cost $1885 by the time he had everything needed to get started.

This chapter covers computer peripherals (a fancy word for accessories), some of which may be absolutely necessary to your computer system and some of which may be desirable options. If you are fortunate, everything you need will come with the computer you buy. That's unlikely, though. There will probably be something you need that costs extra.

VIDEO DISPLAYS

Computers like the Commodore PET, the Kaypro II and the NorthStar Advantage have a built-in video display. Others, such as the Apple, the ATARI, and the Commodore VIC, must be connected to a television or monitor.

Standard Television

Probably the cheapest video display is your black and white or color television. It is possible to connect most computers to a TV in one of two ways, neither of which prevents normal use of the set as a receiver. The least complicated way involves buying a *video modulator* similar to those built into TV games. The modulator is really a tiny, low-power transmitter that sends the signal from the computer to the television. Most modulators use either channel 2 or 3. They cost $10 to $90 depending on their quality. Many video stores sell high-quality modulators since they are also used with videotape and videodisk machines (most have built-in modulators).

Modulators, especially the inexpensive ones, are susceptible to interference. The characters on the screen may be fuzzy, particularly if your computer puts 80 characters on each line. Several computers, including the ATARI, VIC, and Timex Sinclair 1000, have built-in modulators that work well, especially if they are used with modern, solid state televisions.

Some televisions can be converted to video monitors without a modulator, but the change requires soldering a few extra parts on the printed circuit board. Some televisions (those with a *hot*, electrically alive, chassis that can carry 120 volts) are dangerous if converted, both to you and your computer. Beginners should leave this job to an experienced television technician.

Video Monitors

If you can afford one, the best video display is a video monitor. Monitors are specially designed for the work they do, and the results are almost always superior to those offered by a television. Industrial grade monitors such as those used in

WE ARE EXPERIENCING A
TECHNICAL DIFFICULTY
PLEASE STAND BY

CHARLOTTE

A converted television used as a monitor

airports to display arriving and departing flight schedules can cost as much as $1000. Fortunately, most of us can get by with a less expensive monitor. Several companies sell 12-inch black and white monitors that retail for less than $150. One popular small-computer monitor is the Ledex Video 100 which sometimes sells for less than $100. Another popular, inexpensive monitor is made by Zenith.

Today monitors come in at least four different screen colors. The least expensive is a black and white monitor, the type found on several inexpensive computers. The *green screen* monitors are slightly more expensive. They display their data in shades of green rather than black and white. Green is more pleasing to the eye and less fatiguing when viewed for long periods of time. Monitors that display in a light tan are also available. These monitors are just becoming available; they cost more than either the black and white or the green screen versions.

If a computer's video output circuits are designed for use with a black and white monitor or a television set, the computer can be used effectively with any of the monitor types mentioned above. Computers that have color display capabilities need a

A standard video monitor

color monitor to take advantage of the color display features. The least expensive color computers assume that you will attach the computer to a television set, and often make no provisions for connecting to a color monitor. The more expensive Apple II has output provisions for attaching it to a color monitor rather than a television. (You must buy a modulator if it is connected to a TV.) Color monitors are relatively expensive. Prices begin at $300 to $400 for an adequate color monitor.

Some computers, including the IBM PC, provide a special type of color monitor called *RGB* or Red-Green-Blue. These monitors vary in their quality of *resolution*, although all provide a high quality display. Resolution refers to the fineness of the display. RGB monitors, when used with computers that take advantage of their superior display qualities, produce superior video output. However, they can easily cost $1000 or more.

Modified Video Displays

Up to this point we've assumed your computer has the internal circuits for video display, but lacks the monitor. This is generally the case. But what if you don't like the video display system that comes with your computer? Can it be modified? Often the answer is yes. The Radio Shack TRS-80 Color Computer, for example, will display only capital letters. Several companies sell conversion kits that modify the standard display so that both upper and lower case letters appear on the screen. The cost ranges from $30 to $70 depending on the extra features added to the system.

The standard display circuits in the Apple II have some limitations. The monitor displays 24 lines of 40 characters, a format that is not suitable for word processing. You can buy an expanded display circuit board that plugs into the Apple. Your money buys 24 lines of 80 upper/lower-case characters. Similar products are available for the ATARI computers.

Business computers such as the TRS-80 Model 2 always have upper and lower case display capability, but often lack sophisticated graphics features. There are several products that add graphics to these computers. Prices range from around $150 to over $500.

CASSETTE RECORDERS

With the exception of disk-based business systems, almost all small computers use some type of cassette-based storage in their least expensive model. You will hear people brag that their computer can save and load programs stored on cassettes using bargain-basement tape recorders. Perhaps they can, but ours can't. We have around 15 tape recorders now. Some could be classified as expensive (over $70), some are bargain-basement specials, and some we bought at a flea market. All these recorders will work with some of our computers some of the time. Less than half, however, will work reliably most of the time.

There are few experiences more frustrating to a computer user than a five minute program on tape that takes 30 minutes to load into the computer because it took six tries. It generally makes good sense to buy the model recommended by the computer manufacturer or the computer store that sold you the computer. They have the experience needed to recommend a compatible recorder.

Most computers record data on casette by converting the

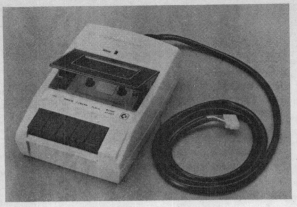

Commodore cassette drive

data in memory to a pattern of tones. Since only two tones are used (often 1200 Hz and 2400 Hz) the recorder need not be a high fidelity unit. It only has to reproduce those two tones correctly. What is more important is the stability of the tape speed. If the motor speed varies, tape speed varies too, and computers are very intolerant of speed variations. Some manufacturers use the same tape transport and motor assembly in both their cheap and expensive models.

When you buy an expensive cassette recorder to play music, the extra cost of the higher priced models goes toward higher quality amplifiers and speakers so that music is reproduced with greater fidelity. When you buy a recorder for your computer, you may want the extra money to go into the tape transport and motor, not the amplifier and speaker. When you shop for a recorder look for the following features:

NOTE: Computers such as the Commodore and the ATARI cannot use standard tape recorders. You must purchase a specially-designed unit that is compatible only with that brand of computer. They generally cost more than standard units, but they also work reliably.

1. Fast forward and fast reverse controls that lock down when pressed (they're more convenient).

2. An accurate counter, conveniently located. If you have more than one program on each tape, the counter can help locate each one.

3. A tone control. Adjusting the tone makes some computers load and save data more reliably.

4. AC power. Don't use batteries since the motor speed may change as the batteries die.

5. A meter (or a light that flickers) which indicates recording-volume level.

6. An AUX input jack in addition to the normal MIC input. The MIC or microphone input on a recorder is used when the signal is weak. A strong signal, such as that provided by a computer, can overdrive this input and produce distortion. The AUX or auxiliary input is used for strong recording signals. Some computers require use of the MIC input, some use AUX.

We should also mention that the reliability of cassette data storage will depend on the type of tape used as well as on the recorder. There is no need to buy the most expensive tape, but expect grief if you opt for 33-cent specials from the discount store. Good quality tapes from reputable companies should do nicely. Use very short tapes, C-10s if they're available. Longer tapes just put more drag and strain on the recorder's motor. If you have 32K of memory in your computer, a program that takes up the entire 32K can probably fit on a C-10 cassette. Long tapes are inconvenient to use since they take a long time to rewind when you want to record a program on the other side.

Generally, you will want to store only one program on each side of a cassette. Storing more than one program invites problems such as recording over the end of a program when you save a second one. A tape with five or six programs on each side is hard to use because cassette systems have no reliable way of quickly finding each program.

Disk Drives

Disk drives are the second most popular accessory for small computers (printers are most popular). Disks do the same job as cassettes, but they do it faster and more reliably. If you can afford disk drives, get them.

There are several types of disk systems for small computers. The most expensive are the *hard disks* such as those offered by NorthStar, Radio Shack, and Commodore. Hard disks use a solid, spinning, recording suface to store data. Radio Shack's hard disk drive for the Model 12 and Model 16 stores over 8 million bytes of data. Hard disk systems are convenient to use and they are very fast, thousands of times faster than cassette systems and much faster than even standard floppy disk drives. Their only drawback is the premium price tag they carry.

A small computer with a hard disk unit is capable of doing the large computer jobs that were once the domain of expensive minicomputers. However, you will probably not need millions of bytes of storage when you begin using a computer.

For those with more mundane needs and smaller budgets, there are many types of *floppy disk* systems for $450 to $2000. Floppy diskettes look a lot like a 45 rpm record encased in a protective cover. The term *floppy* refers to the disk's flexibility. Floppy diskettes come in two sizes: 5¼-inch and 8-inch. (The terms *disk* and *diskette* are used interchangeably.) There are other sizes, but they have not yet appeared in a significant number of computer systems.

Computers that use the 5¼-inch disk cost several hundred dollars less, but the 8-inch disks can store as much as three times more data on each diskette. Disks are available in single, double, or quad density and in formats that use one (single-sided) or both (double-sided) sides of a disk. Double density systems record the data more densely or tightly on each disk for increased storage capacity. Quad density systems put even

A hard disk drive with its printed circuit board removed

more data in each portion of the diskette. Disk drives that use both sides of the diskette naturally have a larger capacity.

Data stored on disks is divided into *tracks* on the disk. The tracks are divided into individual sectors. A 37-track, 5¼-inch single density disk system will store 5 to 10K less data than a 40-track single density disk.

With all the options available, buying a disk system for a computer can be harder than buying a cone at Baskin-Robbins. There are four major factors to consider: compatibility, capacity, reliability, and software availability. Most of the major disk manufacturers produce reliable products. However, be sure that the disk you're considering is compatible with your computer.

A disk system consists of the controller circuits, the disk drive itself, and the software for the system. It is possible to buy a single density, single-sided disk drive for an IBM PC for as little as $200. But you still need the control circuits for the disk drive. That may cost another $200 to $400. Then there's the disk operating system—the software that makes it all work. A DOS (disk operating system) for the IBM PC, if purchased separately, can cost as much as $175. (Note: Some low-priced disk drives don't include the power supply or the case so don't assume a great bargain advertised in a magazine comes with power supply and case unless the ad says it does.)

You don't necessarily have to buy all the parts of a disk drive separately, however. The manufacturers of most small computers offer complete disk drive packages that give you everything you need at one price. In addition, many after-market manufacturers sell disk drive packages for popular computers such as the Apple II, Radio Shack, ATARI, and IBM PC computers. VR Data and Percom have strong reputations for quality and low cost in the disk drive add-on market.

You may have to add memory to your computer when you add a disk drive. Some systems store their DOS in the computer's memory while the computer is in use. If a DOS takes up 16K of memory in a computer that has only 16K in the first place, there isn't room for anything else.

Now, what about capacity? You may find you can get along nicely with a minimum capacity disk system. Since such systems generally cost less, there is no need to buy a larger system. A run-of-the-mill single density, single-sided 5¼-inch disk

Commodore dual disk drive

system will give you at least 80 or 90K of storage on each disk; double density systems will provide at least 160K.

Other applications may call for more capacity per disk or the addition of extra disk drives to increase capacity. Most disk systems permit the addition of three or four disk drives without adding extra controller boards or software. We suggest that you determine the capacity you need, allow for future expansion (add 25 percent perhaps), and then look for something with at least that capacity.

Another important feature of disk systems is their software compatibility. A few of the disk units sold by companies other than the original manufacturer of the computer will not run the software designed for the computer's standard disk system. That means you may have a disk drive attached to the computer that is not compatible with most of the software you plan to use. If you plan to buy a disk system from an add-on supplier, be sure it emulates precisely the standard drive for the computer.

One final point about disk drives. If you are planning to use several computers in one location (e.g., an office with several word processing stations or a classroom with ten or twenty computers) it is generally possible to *network* several computers together. Networking allows different computers to share disk drives and printers. Networking can substantially reduce the cost of computers when you plan to have several in one location. In addition, many of the more expensive business computer systems have *multi-user* capabilities. That is, one computer with a hard disk or several floppy disks can be connected to a number of inexpensive terminals and used by several people at once.

MEMORY

Regardless of the amount of memory that comes with the computer, it won't be long before you'll need more. Whatever you can do with the memory capacity you have, there will always be times when you could do more if only you had more memory.

Buying memory can be confusing for the novice. In one recent issue of a magazine, the advertised price of 16K of memory ranged from $16 to $399. Why the difference? First, the $16 price was for a set of eight memory chips that plug into sockets on computers like the Apple. These computers all allow for some memory expansion in the basic computer. Since the sockets are already there, all you have to do is plug the memory chips into the sockets. The $399 price was for a *memory board* which contains much more than the memory chips themselves. When adding memory to some computers it is necessary to add several control circuits in addition to the chips. Computers from Heath and IBM, for example, use memory boards that are inserted into slots in the computer. These boards naturally cost more.

There are other reasons for the differences in the price of memory. The price for eight memory chips (16K) for the TRS-80 Model III ranges from $8 to around $50. Do you get the same quality for $8 that you get for $50? Some stores and mail order suppliers swear you do, and claim that the difference in price is due solely to the greediness of those who charge the most. In some cases that may be true. It is possible, however, to get *seconds* in memory chips, and it does appear that some of the companies who sell memory at cut-rate prices do so by selling chips that are substandard.

Memories differ in the speed at which they can operate. *Slow* memory chips in a *fast* computer can cause all sorts of trouble. Therefore, exercise caution when buying memory at a price that seems unbelievably low.

There is another reason to be careful. The original manufacturer of a computer will usually charge the most for extra memory. Radio Shack's price for 16K of memory for the Model III was $99 in their 1982 computer catalog. We paid $9 each for two sets of 16K in 1982. The difference in price was $180! In 1982, the Commodore PET computer with 16K of memory (the 4016) was priced at amost $300 less than the PET 4032 which has 32K of memory. Yet the same $9 set of chips fits the PET as well (although you must remove the solder that covers the holes where the chips are installed and change several jumper wires on the board). In both instances, adding memory ourselves required removing the case on the computer and, for the PET, making some changes on the computer's circuit board. That introduces the possibility of damaging the computer, and it usually voids your warranty, something most people don't want to do. We added extra memory from *non-approved* sources because of the price difference between the manufacturer and other suppliers. However, it would be wise to consider the consequences if the cheap memory turns out to be flaky, or if you need repairs on the computer.

Adding memory is not so risky with computers such as the ATARI and the IBM PC. For these computers, memory expansion is a matter of plugging in a circuit card. The warranty is not voided, and there is nothing to cut, solder, or modify. Since the IBM PC is capable of using over 500K of memory, it is possible to save hundreds of dollars by adding non-IBM memory to the computer. The ATARI 800 can only accept

48K of memory in its memory slots, and ATARI sells only 16K memory boards. However, several other companies sell 48K boards that plug into a slot normally used for a 16K board. That leaves two slots in the computer available for other types of accessories.

Mention of the IBM PC's ability to use over 500K of RAM leads to a final point about memory. Most of the small computers that have been on the market for several years can only use a maximum of 64K of memory. Some of that 64K is generally occupied by ROM. Newer models have the capacity to use 128K, 256K, or even 800K of memory. If the way you plan to use your computer calls for large amounts of memory space (e.g., inventory control, mailing list maintenance, writing books) you may want to shop for a newer computer that has the ability to use more than 64K of memory.

When considering memory capacity, beware of fast-talking salespeople who answer questions about memory evasively or with doubletalk. Some ads claim that a computer has 64K of memory, implying that there is 64K of RAM, ready for use. Actually, the computer may tie up 16K with permanent ROM and another 16K to 24K with the disk operating system. Thus, a 64K computer may have only 24K of *user-available* RAM while a computer advertised as having 32K of RAM may actually give you 32K of user-available RAM. The Commodore computers are a good example. Their disk drives are intelligent,

A 16K memory board

and their BASIC language is in ROM (with a disk operating system). There is no need to load a DOS into memory on the Commodore machines, so you have all 32K to use yourself.

However, the Commodore 4000 and 8000 computers are good examples of another problem. It is possible to buy an extra memory board for these machines that brings your total RAM capacity up to 96K. Unfortunately, the 4000 and 8000 series use a computer chip that can use only 64K of memory (RAM and ROM combined). The extra memory is ignored by most existing programs, and is useful primarily to programmers who can write their own software.

I/O

Suppose you've finally scraped enough money together to buy that cute little $595 printer that's been giving you the eye every time you walk past the window of the local computer store. The ad says it will work with your computer, so you assume that $595 is the price of adding the power of print to your system. That may or may not be true.

If the printer has a standard *serial* or *parallel* interface your computer must have the same standard serial or parallel interface; it must have the same type of *I/O* or *input/output* capability. Most computers can be connected to serial or parallel printers, but the capability is not necessarily a part of the basic computer system. It may cost extra.

The Zenith Z-89 has two 25-pin connectors. One of these is a serial I/O port which can be used to connect a serial printer to the computer. Since most serial printers use the standard 25-pin connector, it is very likely that the Z-89 can be connected to a particular printer with no more effort than buying the correct cable, plugging the printer in, and setting a few switches to the correct position (your dealer will help with this).

Even if the printer uses a parallel interface, the work required to interface it will probably be minimal, as long as there is a parallel I/O port on the computer. Several business-oriented computers, including the TRS-80 Model 12, provide both serial and parallel I/O ports as standard equipment.

The ATARI and Apple II computers do not have parallel and serial I/O ports as standard equipment. Serial and/or parallel ports can be added to the Apple computer by adding additional boards to the system. They plug in conveniently, but can be costly. The ATARI computer uses an extra-cost expansion box that costs around $160. It has one parallel port and four serial ports. Fortunately for computer owners, there are some very crafty entrepreneurs in the computer field who find ways to cut the cost of I/O for computers that don't have the I/O capacity you need. You will find ads for all sorts of serial and parallel I/O ports in current issues of the computer magazines.

In addition, several companies sell devices called printer buffers that are handy if you use your printer often. If you want a printed copy of a very long program or a report that is fifteen or twenty pages long, the normal procedure is to tell the computer to list or print the material on the printer. The computer then sends data to the printer at a speed the printer can handle, usually somewhere between 16 characters a second and 150 characters a second. Even at relatively fast speeds, the computer will be tied up for a long time because printers cannot print data as fast as computers can transmit data. The computer must do a lot of waiting for the printer to catch up. However, if you have a printer buffer it is possible to send the entire program or report to the printer buffer. The buffer generally takes only a second or two to accept all the material to be printed out. It then frees the computer for other work, and sends the material in the buffer on to the printer at a speed the printer can handle. Thus, you can use the computer productively while the buffer takes care of the printer. This process is called *spooling*; it is available as a standard feature on some word processing software and on some computers. It is a time-saver.

Most people find that they need at least a parallel or a serial port. If you intend to buy one or the other, we recommend you buy a serial port since it is more versatile than a parallel port. Modems, for example, can be attached only to serial ports, and most printers come in both parallel and serial versions. However, the serial versions are often priced $50 to $150 higher than the parallel version.

IEEE-488 interface

You may encounter another type of I/O port, particularly if you use Hewlett Packard or Commodore computers. The IEEE-488 interface standard is a superior interface; it is used on both HP and Commodore systems. Unfortunately, since the 488 interface is not as popular as serial and parallel interfaces, there are fewer accessories available for it. In fact, on our Commodore computer we use a 488 to Serial converter so we can use serial printers on the computer. Cables for the 488/IO ports are more expensive but are less prone to interference problems.

PRINTERS

It could be argued that a printer is not an essential accessory for a computer. That's true. Much can be done without a printer. It is also true that for many applications a printer is absolutely essential. For example, word processing is not possible without a printer. Most business applications also require a printer. Even if you don't absolutely have to have a printer, you will find one very useful.

Just a few years ago, choosing a printer was an easy job. There were the noisy, clanky Teletype 33's that dutifully printed out their upper-case-only messages for a price of around $1000. Then there was an assortment of well-worn equipment from a variety of sources that cost $400 to $1200, depending on their condition. Many of the used printers were not manufactured for small computers, and thus they required a lot of work to get them running. Finally, there were the expensive printers designed for use with the big computers in heavy-duty business applications. Companies such as DEC, Centronics, and Okidata were glad to sell their printers to small-computer owners. These printers usually worked well. Since they were built for heavy use they were durable and reliable. These traits were reflected in their cost.

Early small-computer owners were often shocked to find that a new printer would cost more than their computer. Many tried to make do with used printers. Some were successful; many weren't.

Today, the market for small-computer printers bears little resemblance to the market a few years ago. New technology, new companies, and new models have changed everything. It is now possible to buy a brand new printer for as little as $200. Printers in this price range generally print on a narrow strip of paper similar to that used in adding machines, or they use standard width paper but the print quality leaves something to be desired. However, they do print, and the price is right. Such printers are good for printing program listings or for performing small business applications such as inventory control or mailing label printing.

Before shopping for a printer, there are several factors to consider. First there is the method used to create an image on the paper. Some inexpensive printers use a heat (thermal) process. Heat applied to special paper turns it a different color, creating characters where the heat was applied. Others use an electrostatic process in which the top layer of a special type of paper is actually burned away, allowing a darker second layer to show through. Both processes require special paper that generally costs more than standard paper and is often hard to find. Although there are many who disagree, we recommend you shop only for printers that use standard paper. That is, buy a printer that uses the same type of paper your typewriter uses (e.g., single sheet) or paper that can be pin fed or tractor fed (e.g., continuous feed paper). There is more on this later.

Once you've decided upon a particular printing technology, you have four other questions to answer:

1. How important is printing SPEED?
2. How important is PRINT QUALITY?
3. How important is PRICE?
4. How important is the ability to print GRAPHICS as well as text?

These are crucial questions. Suppose you have around $800 to spend on a printer and you already have a serial and a parallel interface. There are dozens of different models priced at or below $800. Suppose you plan to use your printer to list programs, to write drafts of papers that will be used internally in your company, and to prepare invoices. The computer operator is a part-time paid employee. That means printing speed is important, but all the intended applications can be performed on a printer that produces moderately good quality print. The Epson MX-80, the Okidata Microline 80 and 82, the Commodore 4022, the Centronics 730, the C-Itoh Comet I, the Radio Shack Line Printer VIII, and the NEC dot matrix printer are all suitable. The printing speed varies from model to model, but all are within acceptable limits in terms of speed and print quality.

Epson printer

Now suppose you are a teacher and you have $800 to spend on a printer for your home computer. You will use it to print resumes and articles for submission to educational magazines. Print quality is very important. You want the highest quality you can get for your money. Speed is not important since you can always do something else while the printer is working. None of the printers listed above would be a good choice since their print quality is lower than that obtained from a standard office typewriter. In this instance, you might look instead at the TP-1 printer from Smith Corona. Its print quality is as good as an office typewriter and it sells for less than $800 in many computer stores.

With the TP-1, you get high quality print from a very slow printer. The Epson MX-80, mentioned above, prints at approximately 80 characters per second. The TP-1 prints about 12 characters per second. Therefore, the tradeoff in the under-$1000-printer market is often speed versus print quality. (For $3000 you can get both speed and quality.) If there is ever a company that markets a 100-characters-per-second printer with typewriter-quality print for under $800, it will be enormously successful.

Of the four questions presented at the beginning of this section, three have been dealt with already: speed, quality, and price. The fourth question, regarding graphics, may or may not be of interest to you. Most of the small computers used in homes, schools and businesses have some ability to display graphics characters on the screen. That means you can use the computer to create tables, charts, figures and even pictures on the screen.

Some printers are capable of reproducing anything on paper that you can create on the computer's screen. This feature can be very useful if, for example, you regularly create reports that use lots of charts and figures. The ability to print out graphic screen displays is a feature of several printers that use the dot-matrix process to do their job.

TRS-80 line printer

Dot-matrix printers produce letters and shapes by pushing a matrix of tiny wires into a ribbon which then strikes the paper. Each letter consists of a pattern of tiny ink dots on the paper. Printer manufacturers often describe their dot-matrix printers in terms of the size of the matrix used. A printer that has a 5 by 7 matrix (e.g., five rows each with seven wires in it) will generally create a cruder-looking printout than a printer with a 9 by 9 dot-matrix. It is easy for most dot-matrix printers to create graphics characters since each dot in the matrix can be controlled independently.

Although some manufacturers use the term *correspondence quality* to describe their dot-matrix printers, few objective critics would accept the output of most dot-matrix printers as good enough to be used on business letters and the like. There are some exceptions, however. A few of the dot-matrix printers use an overlapping dot pattern to create higher quality output. That is, the printer prints a line of text and then goes back and *fills in* the spaces between the dots to create text that looks a lot like typewriter-produced material. The Toshiba TH-2100H printer, for example, uses a very dense dot-matrix and an overlapping print process to create *near letter-quality* printing.

The Toshiba TH-2100H has a maximum speed of 192 characters per second (that is fast) in its *draft quality* mode (no filling in) and 100 characters per second in its *near letter-quality* mode. Most people who need *letter quality* as opposed to near letter-quality output will want to consider printers that print each letter as one solid character. Several printers priced under $2000 do this. These generally have limited or non-existent graphics features.

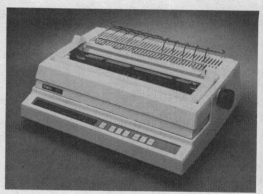

Diablo printer

Most of the printers in this category use the *daisy wheel* print mechanism, which means different styles of type can be used simply by changing the print wheel (the daisy wheel) in the printer. Print quality is very high; in most cases it is as good as that produced by office typewriters. Today, the daisy wheel printers from Diablo and Qume (and the printers from NEC which use a print *thimble* instead of a wheel) set the standard for quality and reliability. They cost between $1950 and $4000 depending on options. They are moderately fast (30 to 60 characters per second), reliable, and capable of producing *letter quality* output.

Over the past five years, printers in the *daisy wheel* group have replaced older printers which were based on the Selectric

A daisy wheel

mechanism from IBM. There are still a number of Selectric-based printers around, and some have been modified so that they can be connected to the popular small computers. Prices range from $200 to $1400. The Selectrics also produce very high quality print, but they have many moving parts and are more prone to breakdown than the daisy wheel printers.

Less expensive daisy wheel printers began appearing in computer stores during 1981, most of them from Japan. In addition, some companies modify electronic typewriters such as the Olivetti Praxis 30 and 35.

We purchased one imported daisy wheel printer which carried the name of a U.S. computer manufacturer. In the eight months we used it, it required four service calls and broke no less than five daisy wheels. At $29.95 a wheel, the printer was not loved by anyone. A well-worn Diablo printer in the same room has not broken a single daisy wheel in four years of hard use. In addition, the Diablo daisy wheels can be purchased for around $8 in most cities. This is not a blanket criticism of all imported daisy wheel printers, but at least some of them appear to have achieved their low price by skimping on quality.

A similar warning should be made about the converted typewriters on the market. The small, portable, electronic typewriters such as the Olivetti Praxis are designed for light use. They are not likely to stand up to the heavy use that computer printers are designed for. On the other hand, the Olivetti 121 typewriter, the Olympia office electronic typewriter, and the IBM Model 50, Model 60 and Model 70 electronic typewriters are all designed for 8-hour-a-day use. Converting one of these typewriters makes more sense. The IBM electronic typewriters produce output that is close to that of a phototypesetter. However, all of the typewriter-printers are slow when compared to a daisy wheel printer.

Some Points to Consider When Printer Shopping

Friction Feed, Tractor Feed, or Pin Feed Platen? Most typewriters feed each sheet of paper into the typewriter by applying friction pressure against the sheet and the feed rollers. Friction feed works fine for printers that print one sheet at a time, but few friction feed printers are capable of using continuous feed paper. Continuous feed paper is one long strip of paper with a horizontal perforated line at the break between each sheet. If you have a 10-page paper in your word processor, it is possible to tell the computer to print out all 10 pages at once as long as your printer uses continuous feed paper. If, however, the printer is a friction feed model, it is unlikely that all 10 pages will pass through the printer without getting out of adjustment (e.g., slipping to one side or the other).

To use continuous feed paper effectively and conveniently, you need a printer with either a pin feed platen or a tractor feed. Tractor feeds attach to the printer over the platen and use the little holes on the sides of continuous feed paper to pull the paper through the printer. The edges of the paper containing the holes can generally be removed along vertical perforations so that you end up with a standard sheet of paper.

Tractor feeds can be an expensive add-on, often adding up to $300 to the price of a daisy wheel printer. Pin feed platens do the same job, but are less expensive. The platens contain small pins that catch in the holes in the sides of continuous feed paper and pull the paper through the printer. Although inexpensive, pin feed platens are not generally adjustable. You need a different platen for each size of paper you plan to use.

If you use large amounts of single sheet letterhead or bond paper in your daisy wheel printer, sheet feeders are available for between $1500 and $2500.

Cost of Supplies. We recently needed new ribbons for two of the dot-matrix printers we use. One printer uses a special ribbon cartridge that was hard to find and cost $16. The other printer uses a regular typewriter ribbon that cost $1.99 and was available at the local drug store. The daisy wheel used on the Smith Corona TP-1 costs around $6 while Radio Shack charges almost $30 for a daisy wheel for their printer. Radio Shack charges $10 for a nylon ribbon for their daisy wheel printer while similar Diablo and Qume ribbons cost much less. Some of the differences in the cost of supplies may reflect differences in quality and usable life-span. In some instances, however, the prices reflect little more than the supplier's efforts to increase the product's profit margin.

Who really made the printer? At a convention recently, we saw a slick demonstration of a *new* printer that the salesman said was being manufactured by their company in a California plant. The *new* printer actually was new only in the sense that the original manufacturer's logo had been removed from the front of the printer and replaced with another one. There is nothing wrong with putting your own name on a printer you buy from another manufacturer, but it would be nice to know the origin of the products your company sells.

The Centronics 737 dot-matrix printer is the same as the ATARI 835 printer and the Radio Shack Line Printer IV. The only differences appears to be in the color of the plastic case and the name embossed on the top. Centronics makes all of them. (We understand, however, that some mechanisms in Centronics printers are made by Brother in Japan.) Since some software is designed for use with a particular printer, it would be helpful to know that your ATARI 835 is the same as a Centronics 737. However, that would allow the consumer to do a better job of price comparison shopping since there may be several stores in your area that sell the same printer under different names. The Diablo 630 daisy wheel printer and current versions of Qume and NEC printers are also sold under many different brand names.

The Epson MX-80 dot-matrix printers is an optional accessory for all sorts of computers including the IBM PC and the Commodore PET. However, the Commodore version of the printer has been modified for use on the IEEE-488 bus. The Commodore version can also print all the graphics used on the PET computers.

Service Issues. Most of the popular daisy wheel printers can be serviced locally in larger cities. Most can also be put on yearly service contracts. Dot-matrix printers are generally not serviced locally unless the local dealer can do it. To handle the service problem, some of the printer manufacturers have established mail-in regional repair centers.

We recently needed service on a printer that cost us $399. We were told that the minimum (and maximum) charge would be $125. Since the repair bill would amount to almost a third of the cost of the printer, we decided to try and fix it ourselves. It turned out to have a blown fuse on one of the printer driver boards. Check out the service options before buying a printer.

Special Features. Some printers have a self-test feature that lets you throw a switch and have the printer check out all of its functions. A self-test mode makes it easier to determine whether a problem exists in your computer or in the printer.

Another desirable feature is a *buffer*. Printers with a buffer can accept data from the computer at a rate which is faster than they can print. The data goes into the buffer, which is actually a special type of memory. The printer then prints out characters from the buffer. If the buffer begins to get too full, the printer sends a signal back to the computer instructing it not to send any more data until some of the material in the buffer is printed.

Buffers also allow *bi-directional* printing. That is, when the print head gets to the end of one line, there is already another line of material to be printed in the buffer. A printer that is bi-directional can simply drop down a line and begin printing the next line from right to left. Bi-directional printing saves the time it takes for the printhead to move back to the left margin and begin printing again. Since bi-directional printing requires the printer to know what is at the end of the line before printing, a buffer is necessary.

Finally, another special feature available on some printers is the ability to print in a variety of colors. Few printers can do this today, and those that do are expensive. However, they are available and their quality is increasing while their price is dropping.

Ease and Cost of Interfacing. Some printer prices include the cost of the cable. Other printers are priced without the cable (which you must have). Cables cost as little as $10 and as much as $50. In addition, the time and effort it takes to set up and interface a printer and a computer vary quite a bit. Some of our printers were interfaced by bringing them home and plugging them into the wall and the computer. Others required hours of research in obtuse technical notes, and more hours taking the printers apart to set switches located in the oddest, hard-to-reach places.

Some printers, when used with some computers, may require you to load in a special *printer driver* program each time you use the printer. That is an inconvenience you should avoid if there are other printers to choose from with similar price tags and similar features.

Number of Type-Styles and Sizes. Daisy wheel printers generally offer at least five or six different type styles. You can change type faces by changing daisy wheels. Some ever allow you to change from pica wheels to elite wheels. Dot-matrix printers can often print in several different type styles (e.g., bold, italic, script) when they are given the correct instructions from the computer. In addition, they may be able to print large double or triple-size letters for headings; they may also be able to print tiny condensed letters that you can use for footnotes. Some can even print letters in a reverse format. That is, the letter itself is left white while the area around it is black. The variety of type-styles and type-sizes available on dot-matrix printers makes them very versatile.

Proportional Printing. A typewriter will take the same amount of space to print an *i* as it does to print an *m* even though the letters are not the same width. Typeset material, such as this book, is spaced proportionally. An "i" takes up less space on the line than an "m." Proportionally spaced material is more pleasing to read. This feature is available on many daisy wheel and dot-matrix printers.

Number of Characters on a line. A standard line of print on a typewritten page contains around 70 characters, while a standard line on computer printouts can be as long as 132 characters. Some printers can print a line no longer than 80 (or less) characters. Others print 132 characters or more on a line. If you need to print long lines, be sure the printer you buy has that ability. Often, the only reason a printer is limited to 80-character lines is because the printer accepts paper no more than 9½ inches wide. Sometimes another model from the same manufacturer has a wider carriage and larger line-length capacity.

GRAPHICS DISPLAYS

For a small investment, it is possible to add sophisticated graphics features to computers with limited *stock* graphics. Radio Shack offers a $500 graphics option for the Model 12 computer that provides it with impressive graphics features. The $500 price includes a circuit board that goes inside the computer, and software that adds several graphics-oriented commands to the computer's BASIC. Several companies sell graphics add-ons for S-100 computers. (S-100 computers are manufactured by several different companies. They all use the same method and pattern of interconnecting different parts of the computer system.) Most of the popular small computers that lack sophisticated graphics can be upgraded by adding extra circuit boards.

MUSIC SYNTHESIZERS

Our first experience with computer-based music was a simple little board that had about $2 worth of parts on it. From this crude little board came a tinny but recognizable rendition of *Boogie Woogie Bugle Boy*.

Today, computer-generated music is serious business. Many college music departments have added a computer to their assortment of pianos, tubas, and violins. *The Computer Music Journal* is devoted solely to computer-generated music.

The minimum hardware, minimum cost and minimum performance computer music systems are still around. Some of them are less than $30. However, these inexpensive systems don't really let you realize the full ability of the computer. (A few computers have built-in music synthesizers.)

A sophisticated music system will cost much more, but the difference is worth it if you're serious about music. One relatively inexpensive system is the Micro Composer from Micro

Music in Normal, Illinois. It is designed specifically for the Apple computer and costs around $220. The price includes a small board that plugs into the Apple, a good manual, and a lot of software on a diskette. The Micro Composer includes an amplifier as well, and with it you can play high quality, four-voice music through a good quality speaker which you

A computer music system

supply yourself. The pitch, rhythm, and timbre of the music can all be controlled and adjusted. In addition, it's possible to compose original music, play it, edit it and modify it, and then save it on tape or diskette for later use. As you compose or play a piece, the music appears on a musical staff displayed on the screen. As each note is played it marches off the left side of the screen.

The Micro Composer uses the keyboard on the Apple computer for input. Two other, more expensive, music systems come with their own keyboard. AlphaSenturi makes the best system. It includes a piano-like keyboard. SoundChaser is another popular unit. Both are sophisticated accessories designed for people who take their music seriously.

HAM RADIO INTERFACES

There are several sources of computer software and hardware for amateur radio buffs. The product of one supplier is described in this section.

An innovative company called Macrotronics of Turlock, California, has created an impressive combination of software and hardware that turns the TRS-80, the PET, or the Exidy Sorcerer computers into a powerful tool for ham radio operators.

The S-80 Ham Interface for the Sorcerer is priced at $149. It can teach you Morse code if you don't know it already, but that is just a small part of its job. When the S-80 is attached between the computer and the transceiver it allows the ham operator to tune in a station transmitting Morse code and see the decoded message displayed on the screen of the computer. It beats figuring out all those dits and dahs in your head. The S-80 can handle transmission speeds from 1 to 399 words per minute. The messages received can be saved on cassette and read later. The S-80 will also transmit code using the computer's keyboard. In fact, you can type in a message while you're listening to the incoming message. Your message appears at the bottom of the screen. When you're ready, just press a key and the message on the screen is transmitted in Morse code. The S-80 has several more features, but these should be enough to whet your appetite if you're a ham.

SPEECH SYNTHESIZERS AND SPEECH RECOGNITION BOARDS

Some of the most fascinating capabilities of small computers are their abilities to generate speech and to recognize or understand spoken words. Speech generation is an optional feature of the Texas Instruments computer, but it is also possible on all of the small computers when a speech synthesizer is connected. One popular model is called Type N Talk. It retails for around $375 and is connected to the computer via a serial I/O port. If you send information to Type N Talk over the serial port, it interprets the data it receives as instructions to say something. It won't win any awards for clear oratory, but it is understandable. This synthesizer will *say* virtually anything you tell it to at a moderate level of quality. Other synthesizers have higher quality voices, but are limited to a specific set of words and sounds that were programmed into it at the factory. We prefer the Type N Talk approach since it lets you use it for a variety of purposes.

A talking computer can be a real novelty in game programs, but it can be much more in other applications. For example, a blind person can hear the computer call out the name of each key as it is pressed. In computer-assisted instruction, directions and prompts can be spoken rather than printed on the screen; this is important when you are working with students who don't read. You could even program your computer and speech

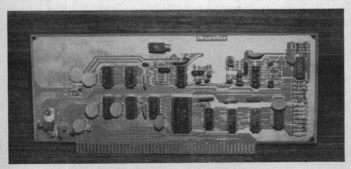

A speech synthesizer circuit board

synthesizer to answer the telephone and speak a message to the caller while you are out.

The opposite of speech synthesis is speech recognition— the ability to recognize different sound patterns. While there are several speech recognition units on the market, their sophistication and usability is not as advanced as the inexpensive speech synthesis systems.

PLOTTERS AND GRAPHICS TABLETS

A plotter is a device that can be used to draw figures and graphs under the direction of a computer. Most plotters use different colored pens to draw designs. Houston Instruments and Hewlett Packard both sell inexpensive plotters. Prices range from just over $1000 to several thousand dollars.

Plotters can create bar graphs, figures, and illustrations on paper or acetate sheets. The plastic sheets can be used as overheads. Few individual computer owners are interested in plotters, but many small businesses and colleges use them because they cost less than a graphic artist to create figures and graphs.

A graphics tablet can be used to create figures, graphs, and tables. However, in the case of the graphics tablet, the end product appears on the screen of the computer. The tablet is generally a special pad about 2 feet square. There is a special stylus or sensor that can be moved over the surface of the tablet. As you move the stylus, it *draws* a line on the screen. You can put a map on your tablet, trace the outline of the map with your stylus, and reproduce the map on the computer screen. The video figure can then be saved on a tape or diskette and used later in a program.

In this chapter we covered some of the equipment available right now for small computers. If we peek over the horizon to see what may be available in the near future the prospects look fantastic. Whether you have a regular task or a futuristic application in mind, new equipment, improved models, and advanced software will probably make it easier.

CHAPTER 12

Where to Find Everything We Didn't Tell You

It is said that an army travels on its stomach. The analogy for computer users might be that their progress is determined by their sources of information. You, of course, are ahead of the game since you had the good taste to read this book. It has provided you with a solid foundation of essential information.

This book, however, is just a beginning. Learning more about computers is a difficult process for two main reasons. First, the field is changing rapidly. In all likelihood, a number of things in this book will be incorrect by the time you read them. Many changes will have occurred since we began writing. For example, the technology of data storage has advanced so quickly that many books written just a year or two ago do not deal with important topics such as hard disk systems, backup storage options, and quad-density or double-sided disk drives.

A second problem that plagues us in this field is the wide range of information available and the highly technical nature of much of it. You cannot become an expert in every area of knowledge about small computers. It is just not possible. There is too much to know, it changes too quickly, and it is not possible to keep all the knowledge fresh by using it every day. The day of the all-around computer user who could write programs, build and repair equipment, and use the computer to do a job is just about over. Most users want to treat their computers just as they do a typewriter or any other office machine. They learn to operate it and leave the repair, maintenance, and improvements to someone else.

Since a computer can be programmed to do many different jobs, it can be profitable to learn something about computer languages, different programs that can be bought and used on your computer, and different types of accessories that are available. It will pay off to spend some time thinking through just what you want to learn. Is hardware and equipment your bag? Is learning to write your own software an interest? Do you want to concentrate on one particular computer and learn everything you can about it? Is there one special area such as word processing, accounting, statistics, or computer-assisted instruction that interests you? The answers to questions such as these will help determine the next step in your learning plan. This chapter will also help by describing some of the typical sources of information on small computers.

BIBLIOGRAPHIES AND DIRECTORIES

There are several directories of computer programs for particular computers. One of the best buys on the market today is a $2.99 softbound book from Radio Shack entitled *Applications Software Sourcebook*. It contains descriptions of hundreds of programs for the Radio Shack, computers. Some of the programs are sold by Radio Shack, but most are available from individuals or software companies. Radio Shack also has a software directory for educational software. Commodore and Apple publish similar directories for their computers and a directory for computers that use the CP/M operating system is available from Vital Information Inc. (7899 Mastin Drive, Overland Park, Kansas 66204).

The magazine *Micro* publishes a list of software for computers using the 6502 microprocessor chip (e.g., ATARI, Apple, KIM, PET, SYM, AIM, and Ohio Scientific Computers). The 6502 software list is a continuing feature of the magazine, which means you'll have to buy the magazine, including back issues, to get an up-to-date list. For some the list will be worth the price of the magazine (available from Micro INK Inc., Chelmsford, MA 01824).

BOOK PUBLISHERS

It is true that some of the big name or general purpose publishing houses are involved in producing books for small-computer users. Prentice Hall, for example, has a number of books about microcomputers, but most of them are written for professionals with degrees in electrical engineering or computer science. John Wiley & Sons is an exception to the general rule. Wiley has a series of paperbacks that are specifically directed to the beginner, with many of them written by well-known authors in the small-computer field. Addison-Wesley also publishes an excellent series of books about small computers.

There are six book publishers who have committed a large amount of their corporate energy to publishing material for small-computer users. dilithium Press (P.O. Box 606, Beaverton, OR 97075), has a list of over 100 books, all of them on some aspect of small computing. The difficulty level of dilithium's books ranges from introductory to advanced, with an emphasis on the beginning and intermediate levels. The dilithium catalog, *Brain Food*, is a free publication you will find very useful. Write and ask to be put on the mailing list or use the toll-free number (1-800-547-1842) to ask for a catalog. dilithium also publishes computer programs for several popular computers; they're listed in the catalog too.

Another important publisher is Hayden Book Company (50 Essex Street, Rochelle Park, NJ 07662). Hayden publishes a variety of books in the electronics field and is an active distributor of computer programs. You will see racks of Hayden software in many computer stores. A similar company that ham radio operators and television repairmen will be familiar with is Howard W. Sams Publishers (4300 W. 62nd Street, Indianapolis, IN 46206). While there are some introductory books in the Sams catalog, many are written for the professional or serious hobbyist who has considerable interest and background in electronics. The Sams books also tend to emphasize circuit design and construction rather than general computer use or software. If you're interested in building your own computer or in designing or building equipment that can be used with your computer, then the Sams catalog will be of great interest.

There are three other publishers, Osborne, Sybex, and Scelbi, which should also be mentioned. Adam Osborne is a well-known writer and consultant who started his own publishing house several years ago. Recently, the company became part of the McGraw-Hill publishing empire and is now Osborne/McGraw-Hill (630 Bancroft Way, Berkeley, CA 94710). The original line of Osborne books were heavy tomes that took great patience and effort (a Ph.D. didn't hurt either) to get through. They were read mainly by a sophisticated audience of engineers and experienced design specialists who were interested in using the new technology in equipment they designed or built. More recently, Osborne has begun to publish some introductory books that may be of interest to the novice. In addition, the company has published several books which consist of listings of programs you can type into your computer and run. Two other publishers, Sybex, Inc., 2344 Sixth Street, Berkeley, CA 94710 and Scelbi Publishers, 20 Hurlbut Street, Elmwood, CT 06110 have a line of books similar to those of Osborne.

Several of the magazines that will be mentioned in later sections also publish books, particularly *Byte* and *Creative Computing*. The management of *Kilobaud* also runs Instant Software, a publishing house with a very nice catalog of computer programs and a book publishing division called Wayne Green Books.

Before moving on to other sources of information we should note that most of the major computer magazines carry reviews of books. A thorough review can sometimes be invaluable in helping decide whether a book is worth its price to you. However, be sure that the magazine reflects your technical level. A very sophisticated technical journal such as *Byte* may give an introductory book a poor review ("it's too simple") while a consumer-oriented magazine such as *Personal Computing* may think it is just what you need. What the reader of a technical journal thinks is simple and what you think is simple might be two entirely different things.

MAGAZINES

We have divided the magazines into categories according to the specificity of their coverage. Every computer user will probably find it profitable to subscribe to at least one or two, and many will subscribe to several. Magazines are excellent sources of current, up-to-date information.

General Electronics

Magazines in this category are not devoted totally to computers, but they have enough articles on computers to make them worthwhile.

Radio-Electronics—This magazine tries to cover many aspects of the electronics field with frequent articles on audio equipment, radio, television (including satellite reception), and video recorders. Most issues include a few *build this* articles. In recent years *Radio-Electronics* has published many good articles on computers.

Several of the articles are introductory and up-to-date, while a few have described ways of building small computers or computer accessories. Since this magazine is on most newsstands, we suggest you browse through each issue and decide whether it has enough relevant computer information to warrant buying it.

Popular Electronics—Like *Radio-Electronics*, this one also tries to cover the waterfront. The mix of articles in the two magazines is similar. It would be difficult to choose between them since both often have useful information. One thing that might tilt things in favor of *Popular Electronics* is the fact that two of the regular columns in it are about computers. "Computer Sources" by Leslie Solomon presents a brief description of new computer equipment and software. "Computer Bits" by Carl Warren generally consists of a page or two of commentary about some aspect of small computer use. Warren may also discuss new equipment or software and may even include a program or two for one of the more popular machines. The construction projects described in each issue of *Popular Electronics* are often computer-related as well. Like *Radio-Electronics*, *Popular Electronics* is available at most newsstands.

High Technology and **Technology Illustrated**—Both magazines deal with a wide range of technology including computers and/or the use of computer technology. *High Technology* seems to provide the most in-depth articles.

Major Computer Magazines

The periodicals covered in this section are all aimed at the small-computer market. They may vary somewhat in their emphasis, but they all try to cover general development in the field. A well-stocked computer store will generally carry most current issues of many of these magazines.

Byte—One of the first, *Byte*, has become a sophisticated small-computer magazine with articles of interest primarily to the initiated. There are articles on programming languages, many articles that tell you how to build computer equipment, and several regular columns on a variety of topics from education to computer languages. Most beginners will find *Byte* tough sledding. New computer users who already have a strong electronics background, however, may find the construction articles both understandable and interesting. In fact, many consider the series of construction articles written by Steve Ciarcia to be one of *Byte*'s greatest contributions to the literature. *Byte* is now a McGraw-Hill magazine that is slick, well-edited, and aimed at intermediate and advanced small-computer users.

Microcomputing—Wayne Green started *Byte* several years ago and lost control of it through a series of conflicts. Green has always been opinionated, outspoken, and somewhat gruff at times. He has also frequently been right on the button with his predictions and forecasts. He started *Microcomputing* after *Byte* slipped from his editorial grasp. Originally named *Kilobaud* it became *KILOBAUD Microcomputing*, then *kilobaud MICROCOMPUTING*. Eventually it became just *Microcomputing*. Green also started a couple of ham radio magazines and has other computer magazines in his stable. His monthly editorial, "Publisher's Remarks," is always interesting to read even if you don't agree with him.

Compared to *Byte*, *Microcomputing* is less cerebral. There are fewer conceptual articles and more "here's how-to-do-it" articles. A recent issue, for example, told you how to turn the Exidy Sorcerer computer into a dumb terminal for a time-sharing system, how to build several pieces of computer test equipment, and how to add inexpensive extra memory to the Cosmac Elf computer. The same issue carried general articles on computers in the office, reviews of several new computers, reviews of commercial software packages, and several more construction articles. Since *Microcomputing* always has articles about specific computers, there will probably be many articles in each issue that do not interest you. The ones on the particular computer you own, however, may be worth far more than the cost of the magazine. The articles in *Microcomputing* range from introductory to very advanced, and the topics vary considerably. There are product reviews, how-to-build-it pieces, articles on different types of computer languages, and actual programs you can type into your computer and run. Few people will be intensively interested in every article, but there are likely to be at least ten or so in each issue of *Microcomputing* that make the issue worth its price. That's especially true if you have interests in both software and hardware.

Interface Age—The cover of this magazine says "computing for the home and business." That is, indeed, where *Interface Age* seems to concentrate. Unlike *Microcomputing*, it rarely publishes an article of interest to the person who wants to use a computer to do a job. Like *Byte*, *Interface Age* publishes concept or idea articles as well as columns on computers in education, legal issues, and mathematics and computers. *Interface Age* is probably the magazine most suitable for the small-business person and the home computer owner with software but not hardware interests. By this we mean the person may be interested in programming the computer but not in building equipment or repairing sick systems. *Interface Age* has articles on programming, it regularly publishes programs readers can use in their own computers, and it has some of the best reviews published. *Interface Age* publishes reviews on computers, computer systems, accessory boards, and software packages. IA also has a large New Products Directory section that includes both hardware and software for small computers. It has to be considered one of the better magazines—the best, in fact, for its target audience.

Popular Computing—The editors of *Byte* correctly surmised that the level of most articles appearing in *Byte* is well beyond the comprehension of most beginners. Not wanting to ignore the needs of a large segment of the market, they created *Popular Computing*. It is a mixture of tutorial articles, product reviews, and application descriptions that seem particularly suited to the needs and interests of relatively inexperienced computer users. Most *Popular Computing* articles can be understood by readers with little or no background in the area of computers. That one attribute makes *Popular Computing* the choice for most people reading this book. That is not to say the articles talk down to the reader; they just don't assume you have a Ph.D. in computer science.

Personal Computing—This magazine covers some of the same territory as *Interface Age*. While the format of *Personal Computing* is a bit less formal or businesslike, it regularly publishes articles of interest to the small-business person. There will probably be more reviews of expensive business computers and software in *Interface Age* and more fun programs in *Personal Computing*. A recent issue of *Personal Computing*, for example, included a BASIC program to print price lists for products with a two-step distribution channel and another BASIC program that let you be Alice searching for the Rabbit with the mean Queen and dippy Mad Hatter interfering with your efforts. *Personal Computing* also publishes many programs for home and school applications (e.g., a grading program for teachers and a program to balance your checkbook). Reviews of new products and listings of programs you can type in and use are *Personal Computing*'s strong points. In recent issues, *Personal Computing* has been publishing more and more articles on business and professional applications.

Creative Computing—This magazine is a lot like *Personal Computing*. It carries articles that can be understood by the beginner and the intermediate. Most issues are a mixture of product reviews, tutorial articles and programs. *Creative Computing* has excellent reviews of computers and computer accessories. It does a good job of reviewing software packages as well. Another strong point of *Creative Computing* is the sophisticated software provided. It has published hundreds of computer games, simulations, and applications programs. Some of the software is just plain fun, but many *Creative Computing* programs are educational (e.g., a program to teach children to solve math word problems) or applications (e.g., a program to help department heads manage their budgets). *Creative Computing* has monthly columns on the PET, Apple, TRS-80 and ATARI computers. These columns are usually only a page or two, but they are extremely helpful to owners of those systems.

Infoworld—Infoworld is different from any of the publications mentioned thus far. To begin with, it is published weekly, 52 times a year, and it is in a newspaper format. *Infoworld* concentrates on two types of information—news and product reviews. The news includes anything from a blow-by-blow account of corporate mergers, suits, and countersuits, to in-depth pieces on new areas of application (e.g., computers and satellite communication channels) and descriptions of new products. *Infoworld* is in a niche no other publication serves. Perhaps it's stretching it a bit to call it the *Wall Street Journal* of small computing, but there are similarities.

If you're not interested in *news*, this publication may still be of interest. It carries some of the most critical reviews in the field. If a new and expensive piece of software is poorly written, if it doesn't do what it claims to do, the *Infoworld* reviewers say so. They don't mince words. The letters they published on one manufacturer told such a tale of horror that many potential buyers changed their minds. To be fair, *Infoworld* also publishes rebuttal letters from the companies involved, but all that butting and rebutting frequently generates quite a bit of heat. If you're likely to be buying a lot of expensive software or if you regularly purchase small-computer equipment for your business, a subscription to *Infoworld* is well worth its price.

Special-Purpose Computer Magazines

All of the magazines described thus far are to a greater or lesser extent *general* interest magazines. As the field has grown, however, many smaller publications aimed at a particular audience have appeared. Some of these publications concentrate on a particular area of application such as education or small businesses. Others concentrate on one computer or a particular type of computer. The publications in this category tend to come and go at an alarming rate, so be sure the one you're interested in is still publishing before sending in your subscription check.

Applications Magazines

There are several well-established magazines which deal with a particular application. **Small Business Computers** (33 Watchung Plaza, Montclair, NJ 07042) publishes articles of interest to the business community. *Small Business Computers* offers tutorial articles (e.g., a guide to small-business computing), articles on special topics (e.g., disk equipment for businesses), and guides to equipment and software packages used by the business community (e.g., current software for mailing lists and labels).

Desktop Computing (80 Pine Street, Peterborough, NH 03458) is a newer magazine with the subtitle, *The Plain Language Computer Magazine for Business*. It is available in many computer stores and some bookstores.

The other popular special-purpose magazine is *The Computing Teacher* (c/o Computing Center, EOSC, LaGrande, OR 97850) which publishes articles on the use of computers at all educational levels. Some programs, usually written in BASIC, are published but the emphasis in on articles written by educators who describe the way they use computers or give their views on the current educational computing scene.

Product-Oriented Publications

A few of the computer manufacturers publish newsletters or magazines about their product. ATARI, for example, provides a one-year subscription to its magazine **The Atari Connection**, to new owners of ATARI systems. After the first year, the magazine is $12 per year for four issues. It contains articles on interesting applications for the ATARI computers, descriptions of new products for the ATARI, listings of programs which can be run on the computer, and other information of interest to ATARI owners.

Radio Shacks's **TRS-80 Microcomputer News** is also a monthly publication that is free for the first year and available by subscription thereafter. It contains product information, fixes for Radio Shack software with problems, and programs which can be used on Radio Shack computers.

Commodore's magazine is appropriately named **Commodore,** and is similar to the Radio Shack and ATARI publications except that it carries lots of information and ads for products produced by non-Commodore suppliers but which are compatible with Commodore products. Commodore also publishes a magazine called **Power Play** which concentrates on home computing, with an emphasis on the VIC computer and recreational uses of computers.

The Osborne Computer Company's magazine **The Portable Companion** ($12.50 a year) also carries ads from non-Osborne suppliers. Apple has a magazine about its computers; it tends to be heavily laden with advertising and pizazz but short on meaty information.

In addition to the in-house publications mentioned above, there are several other magazines that deal with only one type of computer.

Compute! (P.O. Box 5406, Greensboro, NC 27403) bills itself as *The Journal for Progressive Computing* and concentrates on the ATARI computers and six other computers that use the 6502 microprocessor chip. This magazine is one we recommend strongly. It is attractively produced and regularly prints reviews of accessories, programs that can be typed into your computer and run, and tutorial articles that go into the finer points of using your computer. A recent issue contained a program for generating large banner messages on the ATARI screen, a program that lets you use the computer as a terminal, instructions for connecting a printer to the computer, a review of the Music Composer cartridge, and tutorial articles on color graphics, sound generators, and character generators. *Compute!* is not the only magazine that concentrates on 6502 computers, however.

The magazine **Micro** is subtitled *The 6502 Journal. Micro* (Chelmsford, MA 01824) contains articles on the computers that use the 6502 microprocessor chip (ATARI, Apple, PET, SYM, KIM, AIM, and Ohio Scientific). It publishes a mixture of product reviews, construction articles, and programs written in BASIC and 6502 assembly language. *Micro* has grown from a brief offset newsletter with an amateurish appearance to a slick typeset magazine filled with useful information for owners of 6502 computers. Many of the articles assume the reader is an intermediate or advanced computer user, however.

Antic (297 Missouri Street, San Francisco, CA 94107). This magazine began publishing in April of 1982 and publishes articles about the ATARI computers. Early issues have included product reviews, tutorial articles, and some programs. It is a little early to evaluate this magazine since only a few issues had appeared when this was written.

Analog (P.O. Box 23, Worcester, MA 01603). This is another new magazine for the ATARI computers which is very similar to *Antic* described above. It is too early to tell whether one or the other will be the dominant ATARI magazine.

PC (1528 Irving Street, San Francisco, CA 94122). This magazine, subtitled *The Independent Guide to IBM Personal Computers*, is a slick, well-edited magazine that could be a model for others to follow. It carries a variety of articles and product reviews. IBM PC owners should seriously consider subscribing to *PC*.

80-Microcomputing (3838 S. Warner Street, Tacoma, WA 98409). This is one of Wayne Green's magazines. Its format is a lot like *Microcomputing*, which was described earlier. Every article, however, is relevant to owners of Radio Shack computers. It publishes many articles of general interest which are slanted to the TRS-80. Virtually every major accessory available for the TRS-80 and much of the commercial software for it is reviewed in *80-Microcomputing*. Many BASIC and machine language programs are also published, as well as beginning and intermediate articles on using the computer in business, home, and educational settings. The magazine also publishes lots of construction articles. *80-Microcomputing* also has hundreds of ads from companies selling products for the Radio Shack computer owner. It is possible to save thousands of dollars on Radio Shack compatible accessories by scanning the ads in this magazine.

If you've arrived at this point by reading all the chapters that preceded it, you're at least a bona fide *beginning computer user*. We assumed you were at or near a zero level of knowledge when you began reading. Now you're at the upper end of the beginner range. After another book or two mixed with a few subscriptions to some good magazines, you'll fast become an intermediate computer user. Perhaps in a few years we'll even see articles or a book about computers written by you. On the other hand, maybe we won't. Writing books and articles isn't all that much fun. Using a computer for fun, for profit, or for learning is a lot more interesting to most people. We hope you join the millions of people who are becoming informed computer users and that you find computers as enjoyable to work with as we do.

It's a Bit of a Byte
to ROM:
A Beginner's Glossary

Does it seem like the computer industry is a giant jargon factory? Take heart. In this short glossary we will familiarize you with some of the more common computer terms. Most of these terms are defined elsewhere in this book. Others, however, are not. We have tried to include most of the terms that you are likely to encounter in magazines, advertising literature, other books, etc. Please bear in mind that this is a user's glossary, not a dictionary. Our purpose in defining these terms is to help you understand the currently available literature. We have taken quite a bit of liberty with some of the terms and although our definitions are quite usable they are not complete. If you come across a term that is not defined here you might want to check *Home Computers: A Beginner's Glossary and Guide* by Charles Sippl and Merl Miller.

Access time: The length of time it takes for information to be written to or read from memory.

Accumulator: A holding register in the computer's arithmetic logic unit. Used for arithmetic operations and instructions for I/O operations.

Address: A number or name that identifies a particular location in memory, a register, or other data source or depository.

ALGOL: Algorithmic Language, a high-level language for scientific applications.

Alphanumeric: Data presented in both alphabetic and numeric form, for instance a mailing list. The numbers 0–9 and the letters A–Z or any combination thereof.

ALU: Arithmetic Logic Unit.

Applications software: Programs designed to perform specific tasks such as games, educational programs, or business programs.

Arithmetic expression: An expression consisting only of numbers and operators, for instance $2 + 3$.

Arithmetic logic unit: The device within the CPU that performs all of the arithmetic operations; e.g., addition, subtraction, multiplication, division, and exponentiation.

Arithmetic operator: A symbol that tells the computer to perform an arithmetic operation. The operators include + addition; − subtraction; * multiplication; / division; and ^ exponentiation (raise to a power).

ASCII: A simple code system that converts symbols and numbers into numeric values the computer can understand. For instance, when you type *a* on the keyboard of your computer, the number 01100001 is sent to the CPU. (The binary number 01100001 is the decimal number 97.)

Assembler: A program that translates higher-level language code into machine language.

Assembly language: A programming language that uses mnemonic symbols. An assembler converts the mnemonics into machine language.

Audio track of cassette: A separate track of the cassette that allows the computer to play sound through your television speaker.

Bank switching: A software technique that allows the computer to switch between various RAM locations.

BASIC: Beginner's All-purpose Symbolic Instruction Code, a high-level computer language designed for beginners. The most common microcomputer language.

Baud: A unit of information transfer. In microcomputers, a baud is defined as one bit per second.

Baud rate: The rate at which information is transferred. For instance, 300 baud is a transfer rate of 300 bits per second.

Binary number: A number system that uses only two digits, 0 and 1, to express all numeric values. See digital computer.

Bit: The basic unit of computer memory. It is short for binary digit and can have a value of either 1 or 0.

Black box: A piece of equipment that is viewed only in terms of its input and output.

Boot: The process of laoding part or all of the disk operating system so that you can load programs from the disk or save programs to the disk.

Break: To interrupt execution of a program. Most computers have a control key labeled BREAK.

Buffer: A temporary storage place used to hold data for further processing.

Bug: A problem that causes the computer to perform incorrectly or not at all.

Bus: A set of connection lines between various components of the computer.

Byte: A group of eight bits (or a memory cell that can store eight bits) usually treated as a unit. It takes one byte to store each unit of information. For instance, the word "love" requires four bytes.

CAI: Computer-Aided Instruction.

Canned software: One or more programs that are ready to run as is. Many of these programs are copy protected so alterations are not possible.

Cartridge: A $2 \times 3 \times \frac{3}{4}$-inch plastic box that contains ROM software such as BASIC.

Cassette drive: A standard tape recorder.

Cassette: A standard tape cassette.

Cathode Ray Tube: The picture tube of a television set or monitor. This is used to display computer output.

Central Processing Unit: This is the heart of the computer. It contains the circuits that control the execution of instructions.

Chip: A formed flake of silicon or other semiconductor material containing an integrated circuit.

Clock: An electronic circuit in a computer that is a source of timing and synchronizing signals.

COBOL: Common Business-Oriented Language, a high-level language generally used with medium-sized or large computers.

Code: A system of symbols and rules for representing, transmitting, and storing information.

Coding: The design of a computer program.

COLOR: This is a BASIC command unique to computers that have color graphics capability. This command tells the computer what color to use.

Color register: The specific location in the computer's memory that stores a color you want for your program.

Command: An instruction that tells the computer to perform an operation immediately.

Compiler: A computer program that translates high-level language statements into machine language.

Computer: An electronic device that can receive and follow instructions and then use these instructions to perform calculations or compile, select, or correlate data. The primary differences between a computer and a calculator are that a computer can manipulate text, display graphics, and make decisions.

Computer-Aided Instruction: The process of teaching by computer. This is a system of individualized instruction that uses a computer program as the learning medium.

Console: The keyboard and other devices that make up the control unit of a computer.

Control character: A special character that is produced when the computer's control key is pressed in conjunction with another key.

Control key: Pushing the computer's control key in conjunction with another key causes the computer to perform special functions.

Controller: A device that can be attached directly to he computer or to an external mechanical device so that images on the screen can be moved around. A joystick is a controller.

CPU: Central Processing Unit.

CRT: Cathode Ray Tube.

Cursor: The little flashing square on the CRT that indicates where the next character will be displayed.

Daisy wheel printer: A printing machine whose print head has a number (usually 96) of radial arms or petals with a type character at the end of each.

Data: Any and all items of information—numbers, letters, symbols, facts, statements, etc., which can be processed or generated by computer.

Data base: The entire collection of data in a computer system that can be accessed at one time.

Data base management system: A way of organizing data in a computer's data storage (disks, etc.) so that several, or all, programs can have access to virtually any item, and yet a particular item need be keyed into the computer system only once.

Data transmission rate: Baud rate.

Debug: To eliminate errors in a computer program or a computer.

Decimal number system: This is the number system you are familiar with, e.g., 0–9.

Desktop Computer: A complete computer system designed to fit on a desktop.

Device: Any piece of computer equipment.

Digital: A system that uses the number 0 and 1 to represent variables involved in calculation. This means that information can be represented by a series of bits.

Digital computer: A computer that uses a series of electronic offs and ons to represent information. These offs and ons are converted to (or from) binary numbers. Microcomputers are digital computers.

Directory: A list of the files on a disk.

Disc: Disk.

Disk: A piece of flat rotating circular mylar that is coated with magnetic material and used to store bits of information.

Diskette: A flexible disk made of a plastic-like material that is 5¼ inches in diameter (about the size of a 45 rpm record).

Disk drive: An electromechanical device that stores information on or recalls information from a disk.

Disk file: Organized collections of data stored on disks.

Disk operating system: A program that operates a disk drive.

Documentation: All of the available information about a particular computer, computer program, or set of programs. It should include operating instructions, troubleshooting, labeling, etc.

DOS: Disk operating system.

Dot matrix printer: A printer that forms characters as patterns of dots. The dots lie within a grid of definite dimensions, such as 5 × 7 dots.

Dual density: A technique of writing twice as much information on a diskette.

Dynamic memory: A form of semiconductor random access memory in which stored information must be maintained by refresh cycles even while computer power is turned on.

EAROM: Electrically Alterable Read Only Memory.

Edit: To make changes in data or a program.

Electrically Alterable Read Only Memory: A form of read only memory that is permanent under normal operating conditions but whose contents may be altered deliberately by electrical means.

Electronic mail: Personal or other messages generated on a computer and stored in the memory of another computer at a different location. The computers are connected via phone lines.

EPROM: Erasable Programmable Read Only Memory.

Erasable Programmable Read Only Memory: A form of read only memory that is permanent under normal operating conditions but whose contents may be altered deliberately by use of ultraviolet light.

Execute: To run a computer program or part of a program.

Expression: A combination of numbers, variables and operators that can be evaluated to a single number of variable. For instance, $2 + 3$, $A + B$, and $A + 3$ are all expressions.

External memory: Mass storage.

Field: A unit of information that serves as a building block for a record.

File: An organized collection of related records. A payroll file would have a complete payroll record on each employee.

File management subsystem: A program that controls operations performed on a file.

Filespec: File Specification.

Firmware: Operating software that is permanently written to a ROM.

Floppy disk: A flexible mylar disk coated with magnetic recording material on which computer data may be stored.

FMS: File management subsystem.

Formatting: The process of organizing a diskette into tracks and sectors so that the computer can write to it.

FORTRAN: FORmula TRANslation. A high-level computer language used for mathematical or engineering applications.

Function key: A keyboard key that tells the computer to perform a specific action; e.g., the *ESC* key tells the computer to escape the current program and free the computer for other uses.

Gate: An electronic circuit with two or more inputs and a single output.

Graphics: The ability of a computer to show pictures, line drawings, special characters, etc., on the CRT or printer.

Graphics plotter: A special printer that is capable of drawing figures, like drawings and other computer graphics.

Hard copy: A copy of the computer's output printed on paper.

Hard disk: A rotating mass storage device that uses a rigid disk made of a hard plastic-like material. It has many times the storage capacity of a diskette.

Hard-sectored disk: A disk that has the tracks and sectors physically defined. A hard-sectored disk has a group of holes that define the sectors.

Hardware: All of the various physical components of a computer system; e.g., the computer itself, the printer, and the monitor.

High-level Language: A computer language that uses simple English words to represent computer commands. For instance, the command RUN in BASIC tells the computer to run a program.

Home computer: Microcomputer.

IC: Integrated circuit.

Increment: Increase in value by one or more.

Initialize: To set a program element or hardware device to an initial quantity (usually zero).

Input: To transfer data from the keyboard, a diskette or a cassette to RAM.

Input device: A device used to enter information into a computer.

Input-Output: The process of entering data into a computer or taking it out.

Input-output device: A device that can either put information into or take information out of a computer.

Instruction: Properly coded information that causes the computer to perform certain operations.

Integrated circuit: A group of components that form a complete miniaturized electronic circuit consisting of a number of transistors plus associated circuits. These components are fabricated together on a single piece of semiconductor material.

Interactive: A computer system that responds immediately to user input.

Interface: A device that allows other devices to communicate with each other.

Inverse video: A process that shows dark text on a light background on your CRT. Normally light text is shown on a dark background.

I/O: Input/Output.

I/O device: Input/output device.

Jack: A plug socket on a computer.

Joystick controller: A two-inch by two-inch black box with a movable plastic stick in the top of it. When attached to the computer, the stick makes objects move around on the screen.

K: When used as a measure of computer memory, K is an abbreviation for Kilobyte. It is also an abbreviation for Kilo.

Keyboard: An input device usually consisting of a standard typewriter-style set of keys and various special keys.

Keypad: An input device usually consisting of the numbers 0–9 and a period.

Kilo: A prefix meaning 1000. It is abbreviated K.

Kilobyte: 1024 bytes. Thus 4K of memory is about 4000 bytes of memory. (It is exactly 4096 bytes, but 4K is a convenient way to keep track of it.)

Language: It means the same thing as human language. The difference is that a computer language allows humans to communicate with a computer.

Light pen: A hand-held, light-sensitive device that allows a human operator to write graphic information on the screen. The information is also written into RAM.

Lineno: Line number.

Line number: A number that defines a line of programming in a high-level language. Each line of the program begins with a line number. The computer executes the program in line number order starting with the lowest number.

Logic: A systematized interconnection of devices in a computer circuit that cause it to perform certain functions.

Logical expression: An expression, such as A = B, composed of two arithmetic or string expressions separated by a logical operator. This is very useful in programming when you want the computer to make decisions. For example, assume you want the computer to count to ten and then print hello. You could use the expression IF A>9 THEN PRINT "HELLO".

Logical operator: A symbol that tells the computer to make a comparison. These operators include > greater than, < less than, and = equals.

Logo: A high-level language designed at MIT for use in educational settings.

Loop: A series of programming instructions that repeat. The last instruction in the loop tells the computer to return to the first instruction. Intentional loops have some means of escape built into them. Unintentional loops, caused by programmer error, can only be stopped by pressing the break key or turning the computer off.

Low-level language: A computer language at the machine-language level (a pattern of pure binary coding) or somewhat higher. It is neither simple nor obvious for a human being to read, understand or use. Compare with high-level language.

Machine language: The lowest level language. It is a pattern of binary coding that tells the computer what to do.

Mail merging: A software technique, usually used with word processing, that allows you to insert names and addresses into a group of documents. All you have to do is load the disk with the names and the document; everything else is automatic.

Mainframe computer: A large expensive computer generally used for data processing in large corporations, government installations, etc. Ordinarily, the term referred to the extensive array of large rack and panel cabinets that held the thousands of vacuum tubes of the early computers.

Mass storage: The files of computer data that are stored on media other than the computer's main memory (RAM). Examples are diskettes and cassettes.

Matrix printer: Dot matrix printer.

Matrix variable: Subscripted variable.

Mega: A prefix meaning one million.

Memory: The internal hardware in the computer that stores information for further use.

Menu: A display shown on the CRT that gives you a list of options. You select an option by typing a letter or number and pressing return.

Microcomputer: A fully operational small computer that uses a microprocessor as its CPU.

Microprocessor: A central processing unit contained on a single chip.

Minifloppy: 5¼-inch diskette.

Minidisk: 5¼-inch diskette.

Minicomputer: A small computer based on large computer technology.

Mnemonic: A technique or symbol designed to aid the human memory. Mnemonics and mnemonic code mean essentially the same thing.

Mnemonic code: A system of abbreviations, acronyms, and symbols designed to replace obscure, complex terms used in preparing assembly language programs.

Modeling: A partial simulation of real or possible situations.

Modem: A modulating and demodulating device that enables computers to communicate over telephone lines.

Monitor: A television receiver or CRT device used to display computer output.

Nano: One billionth.

Nanosecond: One billionth of a second.

Null string: A string without any characters in it.

Numeric data: Data consisting entirely of numbers.

Operating System: A set of computer programs devoted to the operation of the computer itself, which must be present in the computer before applications programs can be loaded or expected to work.

OS: Operating system.

Output: Information or data transferred from the internal memory of the computer to some external device, such as a CRT, a mass storage device, or a printer.

Output device: A device used to take information out of a computer.

Packaged software: Canned software.

Parallel: The performance of two or more operations or functions simultaneously. For instance, a parallel port accepts all eight bits of byte at one time. This is the opposite of a serial port that accepts only one bit at a time.

Pascal: A powerful high-level computer language for business and general use. Named for French mathematician and philosopher Blaise Pascal (1623–1662).

PEEK: A BASIC command that tells the computer to look into a specific location in the computer's memory and see what is stored there.

Peripheral: Any I/O device. A printer for instance.

Personal computer: Microcomputer.

PILOT: This is an easy to learn, high-level language designed for use by novice computer users. Primarily intended for educational settings.

Pixel: A picture element that is one point on a screen. The size of the pixel depends on the computer graphics mode being used and the resolution capabilities of the CRT screen.

POKE: A BASIC command that tells the computer to put a new number into a specific location in the computer's memory.

Port: A point of access to a computer.

Power Supply: A device, consisting of a transformer and other components, that converts household current (115 or 230 volt) to the voltage used by a computer.

PRINT: A command to the computer that tells it to display something on the screen or print it out on a printer.

Printer: A device for producing paper copies (hard copy) of the data output by a computer.

Program: An organized group of instructions that tells the computer what to do. The program must be in a language the computer understands.

Program recorder: Cassette drive.

Programmable Read Only memory: A read only memory whose contents can be altered by use of electronic signals.

PROM: Programmable Read Only Memory.

Prompt: A symbol, usually a question mark, appearing on the screen that asks you to enter information.

QWERTY: An abbreviation used to indicate a standard typewriter-style keyboard. The first six letters in the third row of a standard keyboard are QWERTY.

RAM: Random Access Memory.

Random Access Memory: This is the read-write memory available for use in the computer. Through random access the computer can retrieve or deposit information instantly at any memory address.

Read: The act of taking data from a storage device, such as a diskette, and putting it in the computer's memory.

Read Only Memory: A memory device that has permanently stored infromation. The contents of this memory are set as part of the manufacturing process.

Read/Write memory: A computer memory that you can put data into or take data out of at any time.

Record: An organized block of data, such as all of the payroll information on one person.

Register: A small temporary storage device in the computer. It holds data that the computer is going to use. For instance, a color register holds an assigned color.

Resolution: The number of points (or pixels) you can put on a television screen (or monitor) both vertically and horizontally.

Reverse video: Inverse video.

ROM: Read Only Memory.

SAVE: A command that tells the computer to store the

contents of memory on some other media, such as a diskette or cassette.

Screen: A CRT or television screen.

Sector: The smallest block of data that can be written to or read from a disk file.

Semiconductor: A metal or other material (silicon, for example) with properties between those of conductors and insulators. Its electrical resistance can be changed by electricity, light, or heat.

Serial: A group of events that happen one at a time in sequence. For instance, a serial interface reads in a byte one bit at a time. Also, magazines are called serials because they are published one at a time on a regular basis.

SETCOLOR: A BASIC command that tells the computer what hue and luminance will be used with a particular color.

Silicon: A nonmetallic chemical element resembling carbon. It is more abundant in nature than any element except oxygen. It is used in the manufacture of transistors, solar cells, etc. It combines with oxygen to form several common minerals such as quartz and sand.

Soft sector: A method of making sectors on a disk using information written on the disk. A soft-sectored disk must be formatted before it can be used.

Software: The programs and data used to control a computer.

Sort program: A program that arranges data in a file in a logical or defined sequence (alphabetically, for instance).

SOUND: A BASIC command that tells the computer to generate musical notes and sounds through the audio system of your monitor.

Special character: A character displayed by the computer that is not a letter or a number; a heart, for instance.

Static memory: A type of random access memory whose contents are stable as long as the computer is operating. It does not have to be refreshed. Compare with dynamic memory.

String: String variable.

String variable: A sequential set of letters, numbers and/or characters. It always ends with a $. For instance, if you wanted the computer to remember your name, you could tell the computer A2$ = "your name."

Subroutine: A part of a program that can be executed by a single statement. This is especially useful when you want several parts of a program to do the same thing numerous times.

Subscript: A small letter or symbol written below the half line. For instance, the 2 in H_2O.

Superscript: A small letter or symbol written above the half line. For instance, the R in ATARI®.

System: All of the various hardware components that make the computer usable; e.g., the computer, the printer, the modem, and the disk drive.

Terminal: A keyboard and CRT mounted together in the same box. A terminal is a combined input-output device. A printer that incorporates a typewriter-style keyboard is also a terminal when used with a computer, or a teleprinter when used or considered by itself.

Text editor: A computer program that allows you to change or modify the contents of memory. It can modify either data or programs.

Time-sharing: A software capability that allows several people to use a computer at one time. Generally applied to large computer systems.

User Friendly: A user friendly computer system or software package is easy for novice users to use and understand.

User's manual: A book or notebook that describes how to use a particular piece of equipment or software.

Variable: A quantity that can assume any of a given set of values. For instance, assume A is a variable whose value is 1. If you add 3 to it, its value becomes 4.

Volatile memory: As used with computers, volatile means that the memory loses its contents when the computer is turned off.

Window: A portion of the CRT display devoted to a specific purpose.

Word: A minimum storage element in a computer memory and the smallest data element worked on by the CPU. Word sizes vary with the design of the computer, varying from eight bits to 12, 16, 32 and 64 bits.

Word Processing: A special feature of a computer that allows you to manipulate text. See also word processor.

Word Processor: A computer program that helps you manipulate text. You can write a document, insert or change words, paragraphs or pages, and then print the document letter-perfect.

Write: To store data on external media such as a disk or cassette. The expression "write to diskette" means that the information stored in the computer's memory is sent to the diskette where it is stored.

Write protect: When new material is written to a diskette, any old material there is erased. Write protect is a method of fixing the disk so that it can't be written on.

$: When added to a letter, A$ for instance, it signifies that the letter is the name of a string variable.

+: It means just what you think, add two numbers (or variables) together.

−: Subtract one number (or variable) from another.

*: Multiply one number (or variable) by another.

/: Divide one number (or variable) by another.

^: Exponentiate or raise to a power.

=: Equals. This is kind of tricky. It doesn't really mean "equal to," unless it is used as a logical operator. In computer usage it means "assigns a value to." Therefore, you might see something like $B = B + 1$. However, if "equals" is used as a logical operator then it means exactly equal to.

>: Greater than. For instance, $2 > 1$.

<: Less than. For instance, $1 < 2$.

Software Publishers

Advanced Operating Systems
450 St. John Rd.
Michigan City, IN 46360
(219) 489-4693

Antic
297 Missouri St.
San Francisco, CA 94107

Apple
10260 Bradley Dr.
Cupertino, CA 95014
(408) 996-1010

Arkansas Systems, Inc.
8901 Kanis Rd., Suite 206
Little Rock, AR 77205
(501) 227-8471

Arlington Software Systems
97 Bartlett Ave.
Arlington, MA 02174
(617) 641-0290

Atari, Inc.—Computer Div.
1196 Borregas Ave.
Sunnyvale, CA 94086
(408) 745-2000

ATMCO
P.O. Box 12248 H
Gainesville, FL 32604

Blechman Enterprises
7217 Bernadine Ave.
Canoga Park, CA 91307

Broderbund Software
1938 Fourth St.
San Rafael, CA 94901
(415) 456-6424

Charles Mann and Associates
Microsoftware Div.
7594 San Remo Trail
Yucca Valley, CA 92284
(714) 365-9718

Cinnmarron
666 Baker St., Suite 309
Costa Mesa, CA 92626

CMS Software Systems Inc.
2204 Camp David
Mesquite, TX 75149
(214) 285-3581

Context Management Systems
23864 Hawthorne Blvd.
Torrance, CA 90505
(212) 378-8277

Creative Software
201 San Antonio Circle
Mountain View, CA 94040

Creative Computing Software
One Park Ave., Room 458
New York, NY 10016

Cyberia, Inc.
2330 Lincoln Way
Ames, IA 50010
(515) 292-7634

Data Train, Inc.
840 N.W. 6th St., Suite E
Grants Pass, OR 97526
(503) 476-1467

Devolopmental Learning
Materials
One Palm Park,
P.O. Box 4000
Allen, TX 75002
(214) 727-3346

Digital Marketing
2670 Cherry Lane
Walnut Creek, CA 94526
(415) 938-2880

dilithium Software
P.O. Box 606
Beaverton, OR 97075
(800) 547-1842

Duosoft
Box 1827
Champaign, IL 61820
(217) 356-7542

Dynacomp, Inc.
P.O. Box 162
Webster, NY 14580

Educational Activities
1937 Grand Ave.
Baldwin, NY 11510
(516) 223-4666

Edutech
P.O. Box 11354
Palo Alto, CA 94306

Excalibur Technologies Corp.
800 Rio Grande Blvd.
Mercado Mall, Suite 21
Alburquerque, NM 87104

Hayden
50 Essex St.
Rochelle Park, NJ 07662
(201) 843-0550

Infocom
52 Wheeler St.
Cambridge, MA 02138
(617) 492-1031

Infosoft
10175 S.W. Barbur Blvd.,
Suite 202
Portland, OR 97219
(503) 244-4181

Interactive Microware
P.O. Box 771
State College, PA 16801
(814) 238-8294

Krell Software
1320 Stony Brook Rd.
Stony Brook, NY 11790
(516) 751-5139

L & S Computerware
1589 Fraser Dr.
Sunnyvale, CA 94082
(408) 446-1657

Lotus Development
Corporation
55 Wheeler Street
Cambridge, MA 02138
(617) 492-7171

Madison Computer
1825 Monroe
Madison, WI 53211
(608) 255-5552

Management Systems
Software Inc.
5200 Brittany Dr. #1006
St. Petersburg, FL 33715
(813) 864-4374

Mastertype
P.O. Box 5223
Stanford, CA 94305
(415) 327-3280

Mercator Business Systems
1294 Lawrence Station Rd.
Sunnyvale, CA 94086
(408) 734-5134

Micro Power and Light Company
12820 Hillcrest Rd., Suite 224
Dallas, TX 75230
(214) 239-6620

MicroPro
1299 Fourth St.
San Rafael, CA 94901
(415) 457-8990

Microworks
P.O. Box 1110
Del Mar, CA 92014
(714) 942-2400

Milliken Publishing
1100 Research Blvd.
St. Louis, MO 63132

Muse Software
347 N. Charles St.
Baltimore, MD 21201
(301) 659-7212

Ohio Scientific
1333 S. Chillicothe Rd.
Aurora, OH 44202
(216) 562-3101

Optimized Systems Software
10379 Lansdale Ave.
Cupertino, CA 95014
(408) 446-3099

PBL Corporation
P.O. Box 559
Wayzata, MN 55391
(612) 473-3769

Professional Systems Corp.
3858 Carson St., Suite 220
Torrance, CA 90503
(213) 316-5345

Relational Systems Int'l Corp.
P.O. Box 13850
Salem, OR 97309
(503) 363-8929

Scholastic
904 Sylvan Ave.
Englewood Cliffs, NJ 07632
(201) 567-7900

Science Research Associates
155 N. Wacker Drive
Chicago, IL 60606
(312) 984-2000

Softside
6 South St.
Milford, NH 03055
(603) 637-0585

Softsync
P.O. Box 450
Murray Hill Station
New York, NY 10156
(212) 685-2080

Solartek
P.O. Box 298
Guilderland, NY 12084

Sorcim
405 Aldo Ave.
Santa Clara, CA 95050
(408) 727-7634

Spectrum Software
142 Carlow, P.O. Box 2084
Sunnyvale, CA 94087
(408) 738-4387

Structured Systems
Group, Inc.
5204 Claremont
Oakland, CA 94618
(415) 547-1567

Syntax Corp.
Box 8137
4500 W. 72nd Terrace
Prairie Village, KS 60208
(913) 362-9667

Technical Products Co.
Box 12983
Gainesville, FL 32604

Texas Instruments
P.O. Box 53
Lubbock, TX 79408
(806) 741-2000

VisiCorp
1330 Bordeaux Dr.
Sunnyvale, CA 94086
(408) 946-9000

Index

Photography Credits

Our Thanks to:

ABOUT THE AUTHORS

Jerry Willis wrote *Peanut Butter and Jelly Guide to Computers* and *Nailing Jelly to a Tree*, and both were chosen by the *Library Journal* as outstanding computer publications. Jerry is a professor of educational psychology at Texas Tech, and is a specialist in the field of instructional materials and methods.

Merl Miller is an industrial engineer who got involved in computers and electronics as a hobby. He is a graduate of the University of Wyoming and has been publishing computer books for fourteen years. Merl has written such helpful books for the businessman as *How to Make Money With Your Microcomputer* and *From the Counter to the Bottom Line*. He is the Chairman of dilithium Press.